# HEAVEN

## IT'S SPECTACULAR!

C. L. MCLEAN

LINCOLN HOUSE PUBLISHING

# COPYRIGHT

# DEDICATION

*This book is dedicated to my father, Bud McLean, whom it was written for when he was 94 years old and in good health at the time he read it. He was sad about the thought of death and leaving those he loves and I wanted to encourage him by reminding him what heaven is like. It helped him focus on the place he was going to rather than what he was leaving behind.*

*Three weeks later, he saw it for himself.*

# CONTENTS

*Introduction*                                          V

1. Chapter One                                          I
*The Joy of Heaven*

2. Chapter Two                                          4
*What Heaven Will Look Like*

3. Chapter Three                                        I O
*Where We Live In Heaven*

4. Chapter Four                                         I 2
*How Big Heaven Is*

5. Chapter Five                                         I 4
*How Soon We Go To Heaven After We Die*

6. Chapter Six                                          I 6
*Where Heaven Is*

7. Chapter Seven                                        I 7
*Who Goes To Heaven*

8. Chapter Eight                                        2 I
*Why This Is Hard To Believe*

9. Chapter Nine                                         2 5
*The Next Step*

*About the Author*                                      29

# INTRODUCTION

Wondering if there is a Heaven or what it will be like after you take your last breath? Many people fear death because of the unknown of what happens next. Fear death no more. Are you facing death or know someone facing it, and you don't know how to ease their fear? Help is here. Sad about the loss of a loved one that has passed away? Be sad no more.

You are about to see what Heaven looks like, and it is beyond anything you could possibly imagine. This is not speculation. It is not my opinion. It is a fact. God Himself showed a glimpse of Heaven to His prophets who wrote it down for us to see. So get ready to be amazed at Heaven – It's Spectacular!

In this short book, you will learn about:
- The Joy of Heaven
- What Heaven Will Look Like
- Where We Live In Heaven
- How Big Heaven Is
- How Soon We Go To Heaven After We Die

- Where Heaven Is
- Who Goes To Heaven

In addition to the physical Heaven described herein, we are told about the joy in Heaven, so let's start there...

# CHAPTER ONE

## THE JOY OF HEAVEN

*H*eaven is a place of unfathomable joy and pleasure! Those times in life when you were so happy you felt like your heart would explode with joy – Heaven's joy is many times greater than that! Heaven is unimaginable joy and pleasure that is continuous and never-ending! The psalmist wrote *"In Your presence is fullness of joy; In Your right hand there are pleasures forever"* (Psalm 16:11 NASB).

No one in Heaven wishes to come back to Earth. People in Heaven are living in utter bliss on a level our finite minds cannot even comprehend. In fact, our finite minds have minimized Heaven and caused us to think Heaven will be boring and not a place to look forward to going. Nothing could be further from the truth. We shouldn't be dreading Heaven but rather be excited to get there. It will be a spectacular existence without any lows. We will be in continual fellowship with those in Heaven without tears, fears, pain, or sorrow.

*"Everlasting joy will be on their heads. They will obtain gladness and joy, and sorrow and sighing will flee away"* (Isaiah 35:10).

Scripture further says God *"will wipe away every tear from their eyes; and there will no longer be any death; there will no longer be any mourning, or crying, or pain; the first things have passed away" (Revelation 21:4).* This may be the most widely known verse about Heaven. There is no crying, no mourning, no death, and no pain. Most of us know more about what will "no longer" be in Heaven than we know about what <u>will</u> be in Heaven.

Unimaginable joy in Heaven is not some wishful thinking. It is not some false hope. This is what Scripture says it is. This is what Heaven is really like. And while some of life's experiences and relationships are rich and rewarding, they will not compare to the experience of Heaven. Why? Because earthly relationships have joy <u>and</u> pain, while heavenly relationships have only joy. Heaven is absent of selfish behavior that causes hurt and pain. Earthy relationships can crumble and end. Heavenly relationships last forever. Even loving earthy relationships can end in death and separation. Heaven's relationships live forever.

Let's not forget about friends and family who have passed before you that are now in Heaven. You will be reunited with them, and together you will bask in Heaven's splendor. And while missing your loved ones left behind may be on your mind now, you will not miss them in Heaven because Scripture says there is no sorrow in Heaven. The focus in Heaven is not on your previous life but on your eternal life and the celebration you are experiencing. Nothing on Earth can compare with Heaven. Nothing!

It's natural for someone to fear the unknown, so in this text, I am reminding you of the known. Scripture reveals information about Heaven so you no longer need to be afraid; you can be free of fear. Although sickness and death might be painful for some, what lies on the other side is triumphant. *"Where O death, is your victory? Where O death, is your sting?" (1 Corinthians 15:55).* Many of us have experienced horrific physical pain or even deeper and more debilitating emotional pain during this lifetime. Such pains will be non-existent in Heaven.

In the book of Job, we are reminded that life *"is short-lived and full of turmoil" (Job 14:1). Paul says, "For to me, to live is Christ, and to die is gain" (Philippians 1:21).* We often get so caught up in our lives that we forget that this life on Earth - be it 70 years, 80 years, or 90 years – is such a small fraction of time compared to eternity. To give you a visual, our time here on Earth is less than one inch of a one-hundred-mile journey. And that is a poor comparison because Heaven is eternal. Life on Earth is less than one inch on our life timeline that never ends. And no matter how nice your home is on Earth, going to Heaven is like leaving the slums and moving into the most spectacular, beautiful place where you bask in an unbelievable joy beyond anything your mind and body have ever experienced.

The apostle Paul longs to leave this life to be with Christ, *"having the desire to depart and be with Christ, for that is very much better" (Philippians 1:23).* We should be longing for Heaven as well. To be present with Christ is "much better". I'm not saying we shouldn't be thankful for life or should be eager to die. Live life to its fullest, and when life ends, know with certainty that Heaven is going to be better - much better - than anything you've ever experienced. Paul welcomed the end of his life here on Earth saying he would *"prefer rather to be absent from the body and to be at home with the Lord" (2 Corinthians 5:8).* Paul longed to be with his Savior. His earthly relationship with God was so rich that he longed to be with Him in person.

# CHAPTER TWO

## WHAT HEAVEN WILL LOOK LIKE

The best visualization of Heaven comes from two books in the Bible: Ezekiel and Revelation. Ezekiel describes his vision of Heaven as it is today – as it is if we died and went there now. John, in the book of Revelation, describes Heaven as it will be when there is a new Heaven and new earth. Both visions are amazingly similar, and both authors are limited by their humanness in describing what they see. Without actually being present in Heaven, they are not able to expound on the joy of Heaven mentioned in Chapter 1, their vision is purely what Heaven looks like.

In Ezekiel 1:4-28, Ezekiel describes a cloud with fire flashing intermittently with a bright light around it. The throne he saw was lapis lazuli in appearance, a violet-blue to dark-blue color with veins of yellow, and a rainbow of radiance surrounding the One, God, on the throne. From the waist up, the One on the throne looked like gleaming metal with fire. From the waist down something like fire is surrounded by a rainbow of radiance.

We cannot fully understand all Ezekiel described, and he did not fully understand everything he saw. What he saw was far beyond anything his eyes had ever seen or his mind had ever imagined. In addition, Ezekiel saw wheels of sparkling topaz that angelic beings used to move about. Topaz is colorless with diamond like brilliance. When they moved, they moved in any direction without the wheels turning in that direction.

Reading this text, you feel Ezekiel struggling for words to describe the indescribable because no one had ever seen what he was seeing. Heaven is beyond our ability to fathom and is a place of inexpressible beauty and grandeur so many times greater than anything anyone has ever seen. The combination of continual joy and the visual extravaganza of Heaven will result in a pleasure we have never known.

The book of Revelation deals largely with events to occur at the end of Earth's existence; however, John also describes the new heaven and new earth that comes after this. He states in Revelation 21:18, *"The material of the wall was jasper; and the city was pure gold, like clear glass."* The wall mentioned is the wall of the city of Heaven, and its color is jasper, which is commonly reddish brown.

The city architecture is pure gold but somehow transparent like glass that will allow all the colors and lights of Heaven to transmit through it. He continues in *Revelation 21: 19-20, "The foundation stones of the city wall were decorated with every kind of precious stone. The first foundation stone was jasper; the second, sapphire; the third, chalcedony; the fourth, emerald; the fifth, sardonyx; the sixth, sardius; the seventh, chrysolite; the eighth, beryl; the ninth, topaz; the tenth, chrysoprase; the eleventh, jacinth; the twelfth, amethyst."* Jasper is reddish brown, sapphire is blue, chalcedony is light green, emerald is green, sardonyx is brown and white, sardius is red, chrysolite is yellow, beryl is a prism of colors, topaz is colorless diamond like, chrysoprase is shades of green, jacinth is reddish, and amethyst is purple or violet.

Heaven is an amazing array of colors and prisms resulting from light reflecting through a constellation of precious jewels and stones, creating a city that is nothing less than spectacular. John lists twelve foundation stones, which are the same number of tribes there were in the formation of the nation of Israel.

Revelation 21:*21-23* "*And the twelve gates were twelve pearls; each one of the gates was a single pearl. And the street of the city was pure gold, like transparent glass. I saw no temple in it, for the Lord God the Almighty and the Lamb are its temple. And the city has no need of the sun or of the moon to shine on it, for the glory of God has illuminated it, and its lamp is the Lamb.*" Christ is the Lamb.

Today, the gates in Jerusalem that lead to the temple mount date back to the time of King Solomon. They are several stories high and approximately 24 feet wide so the potential size of a single pearl the size of a gate is amazing to visualize. The glistening white pearl in contrast to the gold city would be simply stunning.

Some of you may invest in precious metals. Investing tip: the price of gold is going to drop because the streets are going to be paved with it. Twelve gates again are reminiscent of the twelve tribes of Israel; twelve gates, and each gate is a single pearl. There is no need for light in Heaven for the glory of God Himself and Christ, the Lamb, will illuminate it. All these colors and prisms of colors having various transparencies with the glory of God radiating through them create a visual, unlike anything we have ever seen. It gets better...

The throne of God appears in both Ezekiel's and John's descriptions. In Revelation 4, John describes how he was caught up in Heaven, and the first thing he mentions is God's throne:"*After these things I looked, and behold, a door standing open in Heaven, and the first voice which I had heard, like the sound of a trumpet speaking with me, said, Come up here, and I will show you what must take place after these things. Immediately I was in the Spirit; and behold, a throne was standing in Heaven, and someone was sitting on the throne" (Revelation 4:1-2).*

John begins by describing the One who sits on the throne and Ezekiel ends his vision with a description of a physical throne. John tells us the throne is not only the focus of Heaven itself but where the illumination of Heaven comes from. The sun is not the light source in heaven, God Himself is.

John continues: *"He who was sitting was like a jasper stone and a sardius in appearance" (Revelation 4:3).* The One sitting on the throne looked like these two stones in color. Jasper is the reddish brown quartz, and sardius is a deep red, ruby-like stone, almost blood-like. Some suggest that the red sardius symbolizes God's redemption character, the color of blood from the crucifixion, and the offering of forgiveness for our sins through Christ's sacrifice on the cross. Sardius and jasper were also the first and last of the twelve stones on the breastplate of the temple's high priest (Exodus 28:17,20). God similarly describes Himself as *"the Alpha and the Omega, the first and the last, the beginning and the end"* (Revelation 22:13).

It is impossible to ignore the fact that both Ezekiel and John are describing a scene of breathtaking grandeur and dazzling beauty – a glory that far surpasses the limits of the human language to describe it. John, like Ezekiel, is painting a picture that portrays Heaven as a bright, colorful realm of inexpressible colors and dazzling spectrums of light.

Were some of the colors a literal description, or was John using precious jewels and stones he had physically seen to communicate the breathtaking beauty of Heaven? Under-standably, the stones he mentions may be the limit to his imagination, and the actual vastness of colors he simply had no words to describe. Either way, he is describing a place that is more stunning and more glorious than anything he had ever seen.

Sounding much like Ezekiel, John also writes about a rainbow. *"There was a rainbow around the throne, like an emerald in appearance. Out from the throne came flashes of lightning and sounds and peals of thunder" (Revelation 4:3, 5).*

Lightning and thunder are also mentioned in Exodus 19:16 on Mount Sinai when God came down from Heaven to give Moses the law: *"thunder and lightning flashes and a thick cloud over the mountain and a very loud trumpet sound."*

In Revelation 4:6, John continues: *"and before the throne there was something like a sea of glass, like crystal".* It's a spectacular scene with a rainbow of color around the emerald throne, with flashes of lightning emanating from the jasper and red sardius which is God on the throne, reflecting off a sea of crystal.

We are given another picture of the ground when God is present in Exodus: *"Moses went up with Aaron, Nadab and Abihu, and seventy of the elders of Israel, and they saw the God of Israel; and under His feet there appeared to be a pavement of sapphire as clear as the sky itself"* (Exodus 24:9-10). Ezekiel describes it to be *"like the awesome gleam of crystal"* (Ezekiel 1:22). In all three observations, all three authors were amazed by the transparency and color of the ground they were seeing. It must have been breathtaking.

I remember the first time I went to Yosemite National Park and drove several hours through the very arid, flat, bland desert area of central California. After finally entering the park, we turned a corner, and what I saw took my breath away. I took a short inhale of breath out of astonishment. The stunning view of the valley, El Capitan, and Half Dome was breathtaking. The sun's glow on those beautiful mountains, streams, and waterfalls is amazing! The majesty and grandeur of the mountains – incredible! I believe that is the only time in my life that something literally took my breath away. It is like God thought: No one will ever come here unless I put something unbelievable here. So He touched that area in the desert, in the middle of nothingness, and made spectacular beauty. However, Yosemite pales in comparison to Heaven. All the colors and flashes of light and the crystal sea are radiating God's glory.

Ever skied Heavenly Valley in Lake Tahoe? It's amazing. Going up the ski lift with fresh snow hanging on the limbs of thousands of giant evergreens, I looked over my shoulder and saw the crystal blue waters of Lake Tahoe. The beauty was unreal: deep blue water surrounded by a white blanket of fresh snow.

No body of water anyone has ever seen will compare to the crystal sea of Heaven. Combining this with the presence of God Himself and the unimaginable unending joy – no words can describe it. Spectacular times a thousand!

# CHAPTER THREE

## WHERE WE LIVE IN HEAVEN

*J*ohn describes the seats of the twenty-four elders encircling the throne (Revelation 4:4). Elders are the leadership of the church. A Christian is a member of the church, the body of Christ. Verse 6 adds that four living creatures also encircle the throne. Those are most likely angelic creatures, perhaps cherubim which are angels. So, surrounding the throne are the angelic host and the church; occupying the throne is God Himself in all His majesty.

In John 13:31-38, Jesus has just announced to His disciples his soon departure. They do not know of his coming crucifixion, just that he is leaving. John 14:1 says: *"Do not let your heart be troubled."* He is not just telling them not to be sad; He is encouraging them to no longer be troubled, confused, or surprised. He refers to their heart – to not let their heart be troubled. The heart is the fulcrum of feelings and faith. The disciples were filled with a medley of emotions from the sudden announcement of their Lord's departure. They were sad because of the gloomy prospect of living without Jesus' presence. What they assume is going to be a tremendous loss was, in reality, a blessing. Jesus dying was God's plan for them and all of humanity to obtain forgiveness for their sins.

Jesus then encourages the disciples: *"In my Father's house are many rooms; if that were not so, I would have told you, because I am going there to prepare a place for you. And if I go and prepare a place for you, I am coming again and will take you to Myself, so that where I am, there you may be also"* (John 14:2). In Heaven, there are many dwelling places, or mansions, where Christians reside. Where Jesus is, we will also be. We will dwell with Jesus, the creator of the universe Himself.

# CHAPTER FOUR

## HOW BIG HEAVEN IS

*J*ohn is given the size of the new Heaven, new Jerusalem in Revelation 21:16 *"The city is laid out as a square, and its length is as great as the width; and he measured the city with the rod, twelve thousand stadia; its length, width, and height are equal."*

The city of heaven is a big place which makes what Ezekiel and John saw even more amazing because the scale and size of Heaven are filled with all the unimaginable beauty they saw. The city is approximately 1,400 miles wide, 1,400 miles deep, and 1,400 miles high. Try to visualize this. If you walked 20 miles a day, it would take you 70 days, more than two months, to walk along the front wall of the city of heaven. If you drove 55 miles per hour, it would take you 3 1/2 days of driving 8 hours a day to go by the front wall of the city and another 3 1/2 days drive to the back wall of the city. The height of the city of heaven is approximately 8 million stories high. Would that go out of our atmosphere? Yes, which is quite possibly why we are told there will be a new heaven and the new Earth in Revelation 21:1.

That is the size of just the "city" of heaven. Heaven is even larger. On the edge of the city are twelve gates covered in pearl which suggest we will be coming and going from the city of heaven, surrounded by a crystal sea with a plethora of colors splashing off it. Will we live in the city or outside the city somewhere? I don't know, but we are given a glimpse of the outside of the city which is also spectacular.

How can the new Heaven be larger than our current atmosphere? God created Heaven and Earth and the law of physics that govern all aspects of life, including Earth's orbit and the orbits of all the planets in our solar system. Every galaxy and the entire universe is governed by God. God holds Earth in a perfect orbit in the middle of nothingness to sustain life for us, his creation. Since God created the laws of physics, God can also change any of those scientific laws any time He wants, in any way He wants.

Incomprehensible as it seems, we can comprehend Heaven's size but not any other aspect of Heaven; it is beyond our comprehension. There will be a new Heaven and new Earth, and the glory of God is so bright that His glory alone will illuminate all of Heaven with a limitless spectrum of colors and lights, and the structures in Heaven will be built with transparent gold. All of Heaven's inhabitants will experience a joy that will be an unimaginable, unending pleasure for all of eternity. It is a celebration unlike any we have ever seen.

# CHAPTER FIVE

## HOW SOON WE GO TO HEAVEN AFTER WE DIE

*J*esus is on the cross being crucified with two criminals next to him. One of the criminals mocks Jesus, and the other criminal rebukes him for mocking Jesus saying: *"Do you not even fear God, since you are under the same sentence of condemnation? And we indeed are suffering justly, for we are receiving what we deserve for our crimes, but this Man has done nothing wrong." And he was saying, "Jesus, remember me when You come into Your kingdom!" And He said to him, "Truly I say to you, today you will be with Me in Paradise"* (Luke 23:40-43).

Jesus said the man on the cross beside Him would be in paradise that same day. Throughout the Bible, paradise refers to Heaven. This man received the wonderful assurance that he would be in Heaven that very day. The amazing part of this promise is that the inheritance of Heaven is the same for this man, who in his final moments confesses his sin and expresses his faith in Jesus, as it is for a man who has been a Christian for many years.

Somehow this man knew Jesus had done no wrong and confessed his own sin by saying, *"we are receiving what we deserve for our crimes".* He acknowledged Jesus was God and in control of Heaven by calling Heaven *"Your kingdom",* and he placed his faith in Jesus for entering His kingdom by pleading for Jesus to remember him when He gets to Heaven.

For those who believe you have to earn your way into Heaven, this man shows that is not true. He had no time to earn his way. He most likely did not understand any doctrine, and he may have never gone to church/synagogue nor ever read Scripture in his life, yet he is told Heaven is his by the creator of Heaven and Earth.

Whatever you think you have to do or not do to get into Heaven – throw it out. This man's entrance into Heaven had nothing to do with what he had done or not done. It had everything to do with who Jesus was and what Jesus was dying for – Jesus was dying to be the sacrifice to cover this man's sin and our sin as well. That is God's unfathomable love and grace for His creation, us.

This man accepted God's plan for the forgiveness of his sins, and when he entered Heaven, if someone asked how he got there, he could point to nothing other than Jesus Christ Himself. Jesus could see this man's heart, and he was granted the greatest gift of all gifts: eternal life in the most spectacularly beautiful place while living in the presence of Jesus Christ himself and basking in continual joy, continual love, continual peace on a level we have never experienced.

# CHAPTER SIX

## WHERE HEAVEN IS

Up. That is really all the description of where Heaven is that we are given. Up. After Jesus rose from the dead, He appeared to his disciples and spoke to them. Then *"He was received up into heaven, and sat down at the right hand of God"* (Mark 16:19). Jesus ascended to Heaven after his resurrection.

Revelation 18 says *"After these things I saw another angel coming down from heaven, having great authority"*. Revelation 20:1 says *"And I saw an angel coming down from heaven."* The angels in Heaven come down. In Isaiah 63:15, Isaiah requests God to *"Look down from heaven and see from Your holy and glorious lofty habitation"*. God is looking down from Heaven. When Jesus returns in His second coming in Revelation 19 the heaven's open up and Jesus descends.

Whether God is looking down from Heaven or the angels come down from Heaven or Jesus descends from Heaven when He returns - Heaven is up.

# CHAPTER SEVEN

## WHO GOES TO HEAVEN

*G*ood people do Not go to Heaven. Forgiven people go to Heaven. People who refuse to accept the forgiveness God offers are the ones that go to hell.

This may be contrary to what you have heard your whole life in church depending on your denomination. Or it may be contrary to what you have believed your entire life. In our culture, we are told we get what we earn. That holds some truth in business and education but not in the spiritual realm.

The good news is that any person who acknowledges their sin and turns away from it and yields their life to Jesus - whether in the last five minutes of their life or last fifty years of their life – inherits Heaven. No one is good enough to earn forgiveness and entrance into Heaven. It is an issue of the heart. It's not whether you are good or bad but whether you have surrendered your life to Jesus or not. So, this is between you and God.

You may be thinking... my loved one who passed away did not believe this or believed this but was not living like a Christian when they died. So you're wondering if they are in

Heaven or not. Many authentic Christians go through seasons when they don't act like Christians. They may even die while in that season of their life. Only God knows if a person knows Him or not.

I doubt if anyone who knew the thief on the cross next to Jesus thought he was going to Heaven. He was a convicted felon going through a public execution, yet minutes before his death he was assured he was going to Heaven.

For those loved ones who never professed to be Christian, you do not know what happened to them in their final days or final minutes. They may have been visited by a friend that shared God's plan for forgiveness or even an angel – and they embraced it. You do not know. The real question is, what are you going to do with what you learned here today?

The Bible tells us to examine ourselves to see if we are in the faith (2 Corinthians 13:5). When I was younger, I believed in God, and I really thought I was a Christian. In fact, if someone backed me into the corner and challenged my faith, I would come out swinging – defending the fact that I was a Christian, but I wasn't. So do an honest self-examination. And don't worry, there is no amount of sin you have done that God will not forgive you for. To say it another way, there is nothing that you have done in your life that is so horrible that Jesus is unwilling or unable to forgive you of it if you confess it to Him and choose to yield your life to Him.

God knows everything about you and He still loves you. He still offers you Heaven if you confess you are a sinner and yield your life to Him. Just so you know, my sin list was long, and I still sin frequently – but I'm forgiven. Heaven is not filled with good people or sinless people. It is filled with sinful people who have been forgiven by God.

*"Jerusalem, the holy city; For the uncircumcised and the unclean will no longer come into you" (Isaiah 52:1). "Look down*

*from Your holy dwelling place, from heaven" (Deuteronomy 26:15).
"For He looked down from His holy height; From heaven the Lord
looked upon the earth" (Psalms 102:19). "The Lord is in His holy
temple; the Lord's throne is in heaven" (Psalms 11:4).*

All that to say, Heaven is a holy place where God resides.
God the Father is holy and sinless. God the Son, Jesus, is holy
and sinless. God, the Holy Spirit is holy and sinless. Unfortunately, everyone ever born except for Jesus has sinned. The
good news is God created a way for all humanity to have
their sins forgiven so we can go to Heaven. We are not just
forgiven, our sins are covered. Jesus covers our sins so we
can be holy in an all-holy place, Heaven. There is no sin in
Heaven. There are sinful people there that have had their sins
covered/ forgiven by God who accepted God's plan for
forgiveness through Jesus Christ.

When I became a Christian, I realized I had sinned. One
sin - any sin - will separate you from God and Heaven for
eternity if you are not a Christian. Jesus came to die as a
sacrifice for your sin, everyone's sin. Jesus lived a sinless life,
and He was able to live a sinless life because He was the Son
of God yet equal with God. The religious leaders falsely
accused Him because He exposed those leaders as false
teachers. As a result, they brought false accusations against
Jesus that led to Him being sentenced to die by crucifixion.
But Jesus' crucifixion was God's plan from the beginning.
Jesus death paid for our sins so we can be forgiven and have
a way to enter Heaven.

Jesus came to Earth to die as a covering for our sins.
Because Jesus was God in the flesh, His sinless life and sacri-
ficial death can cover all the sins of everyone willing to
confess their sins and give God control of their lives.

Nicodemus was a respected religious leader when Jesus
walked this Earth. Nicodemus thought that to be a forgiven
follower of Jesus meant you did certain religious duties,

acted a certain way, or taught certain religious teachings — you changed your behavior. Jesus said he had it backward. You don't do good things to earn God's forgiveness. Becoming a Christian is the first step. Asking Jesus to forgive your sins and choosing to yield your life to Christ is the first step. God will transform your heart into one that desires to please God.

Jesus told Nicodemus, *"Truly, truly, I say to you unless someone is born again, he cannot see the kingdom of God"* (John 3:3). That means born again spiritually. Becoming a Christian is like God taking His heart and inserting it into yours; He transforms your heart into a heart like His. It's supernatural but real. You don't become perfect, but your desires change, and you become more like Jesus. You begin to change from the inside out. Sometimes the change is slow, and sometimes it is radically fast, but a transformed life to some degree is evidence that you have the Holy Spirit working in you. The change is ongoing over a lifetime. No change in your life shows there is no Holy Spirit in you, and there has been no transformation by Jesus.

*"Therefore if anyone is in Christ, this person is a new creation; the old things passed away; behold, new things have come"* (2 Corinthians 5:17). Becoming a Christian is a life-changing experience. You become a new creation and it's God that does the changing! Not just part of your life but all of your life. You will have a peace that you have never known before. You will have a purpose beyond your work or school. It is not something you do; it is something done in you by God.

Becoming a Christian does not mean you become a perfect person or have to try to be perfect. A Christian is perfect positionally before God because of what Jesus did for you by dying for your sins. You will still sin, and you will never be perfect on this Earth. But you can be perfect positionally in Jesus and that is why Heaven is your inheritance.

# CHAPTER EIGHT

## WHY THIS IS HARD TO BELIEVE

*T*he first time I heard someone speak about having a personal relationship with Jesus Christ, I threw my hands up and prayed – God, I don't know what this guy is talking about, but I know it's what I'm missing. Somehow God, in His grace and mercy, honored that simple prayer and gave me a new heart in Christ. I was transformed, not because of anything I did but because of what Jesus did for me.

Prior to the day I became a Christian, I believed there was a God, but being truly changed was something I didn't even know existed. When I heard about a transformed life for the first time, I knew I did not have it. I was aware I was a sinner and had sinned a lot, but I also thought I was a better person than most people. I even believed in the life, death, and resurrection of Jesus; however, it was more of an intellectual belief rather than a yielding of my life to Jesus. I had not been transformed, and I knew it.

You can believe everything the Bible says about Jesus' life, death, and resurrection, but that does not make you a Christian. James 2:19 says, *"the demons also believe, and shudder."* The demons believe everything about Jesus' life, death, and resurrection but they are not Christians, obviously. What you believe must go from just a head knowledge of God to a heart for Him, resulting in you giving control of your life to Christ.

So what kept me from believing what I should have believed? I was around religious activities a lot but was somehow blinded to my needing a personal relationship with Jesus Christ that resulted in me being transformed by Christ. When I heard what you are hearing now, it was like a light went on and I knew this was the truth. 2 Corinthians 4:4 says: *"The god of this world has blinded the minds of the unbelieving so that they will not see the light of the gospel of the glory of Christ, who is the image of God."*

The god of this world, which is Satan, can blind you so you do not see who the person of Jesus Christ is. You can also be blinded to your own spiritual condition and miss out on the abundant life that Jesus intends for you.

There is not time here to debate if Satan is real or not, but all you have to do is look at all the evil in this world to be convinced. The spirit behind this evil is Satan. It is actually easier to see today than ever before in our culture. What God says is good is now bad, and what God says is bad is now good. If you see people saying things and believing things that you know are simply not true, you are witnessing people being blinded to the truth.

So how do you become a Christian that has been transformed like has been mentioned here? By asking God to do it in prayer. I don't know how you go from praying words that you don't really mean in your heart to praying words you really do mean - that is between you and God. God knows if, in your heart, you really mean what you pray or not. But becoming a Christian is giving up all that you are for all that Jesus is. Jesus taught on what it cost to become a Christian: *"The kingdom of Heaven is like a treasure hidden in the field, which a man found and hid again; and from joy over it he goes and sells everything that he has, and buys that field. Again, the kingdom of Heaven is like a merchant seeking fine pearls, and upon finding one pearl of great value, he went and sold everything that he had and bought it"* (Matthew 13:44-46).

Jesus was teaching in parables which are stories, and the "treasure" and "pearl of great value" represent finding the truth of God's plan for your forgiveness of sins and being willing to give up all that you are for all that Jesus is. Do you have to give all your money away? No, that is not the point. It is giving up all that you are - yielding your plans for your life to Jesus' plan for your life.

You may be thinking you want to get things right in your life before you become a Christian. To that, I say you never will. You can't without a transformed heart. You never will get things right enough for Jesus because there is no amount of good that you can do to <u>earn</u> God's forgiveness. It isn't about what you do; it is about what Jesus did for you. Isaiah 64:6 says, *"And all our righteous deeds are like a filthy garment"* – to God. All our good works are nothing to God. You come to God and ask Him to change things in you. He will do the changing in you. He will transform you.

God's offering of forgiveness is a gift to you. No one can earn it. No one deserves it - not me, not you, no one. Ephesians 2:8-9 says, *"For by grace you have been saved through faith; and this is not of yourselves, it is the gift of God; not a result of works, so that no one may boast."* Saved through faith - faith in the life, death and resurrection of Jesus.

If you could do numerous good deeds to <u>earn</u> your salvation – who would get the glory for that? You would. Jesus is providing forgiveness of your sins as a gift, and because of it, the way for you to get to Heaven to live with Him forever.

Who gets the glory for that? Jesus does. But who gets the benefits? You do!

You may know people who say they are Christians but live a life that does not look like they have been transformed. I know people like that too. I was one of them. The standard for Christian living is what the Bible says - not what people say or do. And the process of becoming more like Christ happens as you learn more about Him and He transforms your heart. The promise of Heaven is a certainty at the moment you become a Christian. The elimination of sin in your life is often a life long process.

# CHAPTER NINE

## THE NEXT STEP

*I* write this final Chapter because I have come to realize Heaven is so much greater than anything we can imagine. No words can even begin to describe it. Everything wonderful we have experienced on Earth is so much greater in Heaven that our human minds are incapable of comprehending it.

In Heaven, Christians will experience an unfathomable joy that is continuous and never-ending while experiencing perfect peace, perfect love, surrounded by the beauty and brilliance of a spectrum of colors and light that we cannot even comprehend here on Earth.

This world was created in seven days with all its splendor and beauty. Jesus says in John 14:2 that He went to prepare a place for us – in Heaven. God spoke everything we know into existence in seven days, yet Heaven is a place Jesus tells us He goes to prepare. Jesus' imagination is beyond any human imagination. Jesus' creativity is beyond any human creativity. How marvelous must Heaven be with Jesus saying He is preparing it?

Human creativity is limited to what we have seen or

experienced. No human has created anything new apart from some version of what already existed. We do not possess the ability to create beyond what has already been created. Everything we have ever seen is a derivative of something already created. Thus, Ezekiel and John are limited by their lack of creativity to describe the limitless creativity of God. You and I are not capable of understanding what Heaven is going to be like because there will be an infinite amount of creativity from an infinitely creative God but know this for certain - it is going to be better than anything we have ever seen or experienced in our lifetime.

The first three qualities listed for Christians to exhibit in Galatians 5:22 are love, joy, and peace. Not only have we never known those in perfection, but also we have only experienced those in small measure because they are clouded by selfish motives and flawed human effort. Heaven will also be an unbelievable celebration - *"a great multitude which no one could count"* (Revelation 7:9-10), celebrating, singing and praising. It will be a concert unlike anything we have ever seen and a celebration beyond any celebration on Earth.

We are not going to be missing anything when we go to Heaven. Heaven is going to be infinitely better than this life. God has given us a glimpse of Heaven with a focus mostly on what the physical Heaven is going to look like. All the other qualities of Heaven are beyond our ability to comprehend. God's attributes in perfection are beyond our ability to fully comprehend.

If God has prompted your heart about anything while reading this book, this is the time for you to respond. Prompting your heart is as simple as what you have been thinking about while reading this. Maybe you have never prayed. Prayer is simply talking with God. Stop whatever you are doing and talk to God about whatever God has put on your heart to do. It is easy to let the busyness of life keep us from doing what we know we need to do. Stop and pray.

Whether you are young or old, at the beginning of life or the end, there is never a better time than right now. If you have not already done it, do it now. Confess to Jesus that you are a sinner, ask for His forgiveness, acknowledge Jesus died for your sins, and yield the control of your life to Him. Give up all that you are for all that He is. Choose Jesus and seek His direction in the decisions you make. It will be the best decision of your life.

If you become a Christian, find a Bible-teaching church to attend so you can learn more about Christ and ask to be baptized. To be baptized means to be dipped or immersed in water. Jesus commands the people in Matthew 28:19 who have become Christians to identify with Him through the waters of baptism symbolizing His death, burial, and resurrection. Being leaned back into the water during baptism is symbolic of Jesus' death, and coming up out of the water is symbolic of His resurrection.

If you are not sure who Jesus is or how you start your walk with God, begin by reading the book of John in the New Testament of the Bible. It is the fourth book in the New Testament. Read a chapter or so a day. Pray before you read, "Jesus, show me who You are and how You want me to live for You." If you do not have a Bible, visit a Bible-teaching church and ask them for one, and they will most likely give you one. May God bless you and keep you on this journey of life. Heaven awaits…

PLEASE TAKE a minute and review this book on Amazon by clicking on the review stars of this book.

# ABOUT THE AUTHOR

**C. L. McLean** is an emerging author whose style reflects his TV and film writing background. His conversational dialogue is bold and direct with authentic transparency and biblical enlightenment. Reading this compact book is like having a living room conversation with the author.

Please take a minute and review this book on Amazon by clicking on the review stars of the book.

It took that one conversation for Jonah and me to know exactly what was happening. We had experienced an eerie "She's back ..." sensation upon interacting with this foreign yet familiar person again. She would nearly incessantly call, FaceTime, DM, and text me when she knew I was off work within that time. Finally, Jillian presenting herself in this declining week's state—stained shirt, noticeably less hygienic, extreme and fluctuating emotions—on Facebook Live was enough to trigger the final warning alarms. Jonah and I spoke with Jenna (sister/resident psych nurse), who practically confirmed our suspicions and helped us speak to Mom more in depth about the developing situation. Mom thought it best that we younger two now completely remove ourselves. Some of us didn't need to be told twice. Hell, he didn't need to be told once.

Jourdan and I took significantly different approaches on how to handle the frustrating bombardment of Jillian's self-perceived urgency; unfortunately, she took the path that generated more content for writing a personal narrative. Whereas Jourdan helped her in the kitchen during the first episode and often answered her FaceTimes during the second, I took a much more passive approach. I refused to eat any of the food she made during the first episode, and I might have answered one FaceTime from her during the second. It wasn't as bad as it sounds, I promise. She asked for me *every time* she called Jourdan, so it evened out.

I had no interest in indulging her conspiracy theories for two reasons: 1) I firmly believed it would not help her in any way, and 2) It was exhausting to me. There were times Jourdan would enter the room talking to her on the phone, and I would give her the "I'm not here" signal. You know the one.

It isn't behavior that I'm proud of, especially now after reading the pain that Jillian had endured, but my mind was elsewhere. I was preparing for my first year of college, which entailed living on my own and playing collegiate soccer for the first time.

From that point on, after her hospital experience in California began, we only heard brief updates of Jillian's health. I returned to my super normal, non-dystopian senior year of high school, and Jonah ventured to Indianapolis for the start to the best 4 years of his life at the dopest, 6-foot-radius-themed parties since the Plague! This time around, we recognized Mom's fear, and when she decided to leave for California, it became clear that Jillian's circumstances were not exactly improving.

Within scraps of information from Mom and Jenna for the following weeks, Mom's return to Indiana and Jillian's subsequent Zoom-viewed wedding (beautiful and definitely never froze!) marked the last of that episode in our minds. Now, with everyone on the same page about Jillian's diagnosis, our age allowed us to participate in intellectual conversations about the entirety of our lifetime's exposure to bipolar disorder ...

# CHAPTER ELEVEN

When I was being admitted to the Panorama City hospital for the first time, I didn't know my name. Was speaking garbled gibberish. I'm sure it was nearly impossible to get anything out of me that was any semblance of rational. To our advantage, the hospital was within walkable distance from our apartment, so Jeff was able to help at least get me through entry.

After that, I was on my own.

Now I have to deviate from the story for just a moment, to give you a brief description of Panorama City. It'll just add some fun little context.

As our shared lease in Koreatown was nearing its end in late 2018, Jeff and I began apartment searching once again and were able to find a relatively inexpensive and roomy apartment to move to. We didn't know much about Panorama City before moving, but we learned pretty quickly what it was about.

Panorama City is a densely-populated, heavily-Hispanic/Latino area in the northern part of Los Angeles County, right near Van Nuys. It serves as a hub to a vast population of MS-13 gang members. This is not a speculation on my part; they make up much of the area's arrest statistics. Perhaps that wouldn't have been such a terrifying tidbit to learn, but I was well aware of the violent nature of MS-13, having read about them long ago in online news articles. Our neighborhood was frequently taped off with that infamous yellow "CAUTION" tape, and helicopters would often drone overhead.

Notably, it also didn't tremendously help that a friend of mine introduced me to a phone app called "Citizen," which gives the user the ability to receive live updates on local events from neighbors. So I was learning, in real time, of every nearby fire, riot, and criminal incident happening within the vicinity.

This didn't exactly do my already struggling mental health a world of good, as I'm sure you deduced.

Now take this bit of new knowledge you've gleaned about the area in which we were situated, and picture being quarantined in it.

*Now take all of that* and guess what the patient population in the hospital must consist of. If you supposed it might consist of ex-cons (assuming they weren't present-day criminals, though I'd wager a hypothetical chunk of money that many of them were dabbling), drug addicts, homeless people, etc., you are correct. Throw little ol' me in the mix, and have we got ourselves a sticky wicket.

Oh, and lest we forget, there were also the great, new, and definitely-not-unrealistic-or-arbitrary, Covid-19 measures of nurses and technicians yelling at me to keep my mask on AT ALL TIMES (which I and most other patients chose to ignore) and not allowing ANY visitors.

It is an understatement to call this chapter of my bipolar journey a nightmare.

I was initially kept in the emergency room, as the hospital was overflowing with patients. I have a fuzzy memory of being in a bed and just babbling. Singing, chatting, yelling, whispering a lilting monologue of absurdity … nothing that made any sense.

Even if they'd told me beforehand what they were doing, I lacked the ability to discern any of my immediate surroundings.

The needle was a harsh stab.

I don't know if substances were flowing in or out. Did they inject me with something? Were they drawing blood?

Couldn't tell you.

When I was moved to a different area, I was suddenly in the midst of patients who all had their own problems and didn't know what the hell mine was.

Neither did I.

I was asked every day by a nurse the same question:

"Do you know why you're here?"

I never gave her the same answer twice, but you know what didn't even occur to me?

Bipolar disorder.

Not once.

Sure, I answered her question. But I answered it with anything I could think of that seemed a reasonable assumption to me: PTSD, anxiety, OCD, the list went on and on.

But I forgot about bipolar disorder entirely.

Jenna—now a psych nurse herself—and my mother would call almost daily and try to walk the nurses through what was happening. They knew.

They (and my fiancé) were in daily contact with me if they could help it, making sure I didn't lose my grip on reality altogether and fighting to try and get the right treatment plan underway. The nurses and doctors chose to ignore their pleas not to administer some antipsychotics I'd had in the past and didn't react well to (Risperidone aka Risperdal and Paliperidone aka Invega).

Meanwhile, I was making friends.

If a giant, durag-wearing man derogatorily referring to me as "Scary Carrie", shoving me around forcefully, and slapping my ass with a towel counts as friends.

If a man with a bald head and face completely coated in tattoos dealing prescribed meds to other patients counts as friends. (He once asked me what medications the nurses kept administering to me, and I replied, "I don't know." He was alarmed by my response, that I would just take whatever they were giving me without asking what it was. The irony lost on him, of course, that he was just passing around medications to other patients without knowing the complete drug profile.)

If the struggling addict sharing my room, regularly drooling, urinating, and defecating all over the place, stealing my clothes and ripping them to shreds counts as friends.

There was one time I was administered an injection. I assume it was Invega, but I honestly don't know. I became very lightheaded; I knew I was on my way to fainting. I recall asking a male orderly for something sugary to drink or a snack—just something to spike my blood sugar. After all, I'd seen him pass snacks and drinks to other patients not long ago.

> "We're about to go to dinner, you don't need anything."

"But I-I'm going to pass out. I just got a shot. My blood sugar is low or something, I—."

"No it's not. You're going to be fine. We're going in, like, 10 minutes."

"I can't—wait—"

And suddenly my vision was clouding, I was leaning, stumbling … thankfully, there was another tech or nurse right nearby ("Whoa, whoa, whoa! Jillian! Jillian, right here."), who witnessed the exchange and quickly grabbed a chair for me to fall into. I waited with my head between my knees as he grabbed me the snacks and drinks the other orderly refused to give.

I remember once waking up at an ungodly hour, sitting outside my bedroom doorway, and furiously scrawling a family tree on a tiny scrap of paper.

I would shuffle through the photos Jeff brought to the hospital for me almost hourly.

I was trying not to forget.

*Do you know why you're here?*
*Do you know why you're here?*
*Do you—*

# JENNA (YOUNGER SISTER/ PSYCH NURSE)

Jeff is able to get Jillian to the ER, by some miracle. And thankfully, he says she was "actually super agreeable."

Words we don't often use to describe Jillian, even in her best state of mind (although we do love her for who she is).

And yet, another sign that maybe Jillian knew something was wrong: She went. With no fight.

Although she may not have been all that aware, I had a feeling that once she had any inkling of reality, she would not be too happy with him. So, I began to prepare him for that because I felt that could be the hardest thing to hear from her at this moment, when he was already crushed. If it happened sooner rather than later, such as in the ER before they even got her back to inpatient, I wanted him to know that for her sake, and his, she needed immediate help. So, I reassured him as best I could. I let him know he is doing exactly what needs to be done for her. She may try to claim it as a betrayal or say he doesn't have faith or "believe in the magic," and it may feel scary and like he is going against her wishes, but he cannot take care of her without intervention right now. I implore him to remain strong and tell him he is handling this all so well, and she is so lucky to have him. And somehow, Jeff was not completely overwhelmed by our incessant texting to check on her just yet. We offered our support and he accepted. I am grateful for this, as for my own peace of mind, I needed to be involved. From here on, he kept us updated, and we tried to do our best to "be there" from halfway across the country.

The evening of July 15th, he informed us they were placing her on a "three-day hold" before referring her to outpatient. During the time Jeff was speaking with administration, he said Jillian "wouldn't stop babbling in tongues the entire time." Honestly, it was probably for the best that she was incoherent and hyperverbal, as this led them to see firsthand that Jeff would not be able to care for her on his own. The rate at which she decompensates is expeditious, and, at this point, she is too far gone to take home and wait for Friday's appointment.

Then, Jeff apologized for not finding someone to treat her sooner, and I wanted to hug and smack him at the same time. He had no idea how much respect and gratitude I had for him. He had done everything possible to do what Jillian would have wanted, trying to keep her out of a facility, until it just spiraled out of control, and he had to do what was in her best interest.

Thus, the 72-hour hold began, and (in my experience) "holds" were only counted on days where the courthouse is open. It wasn't made completely clear whether this was on a voluntary or involuntary basis, but I suspected it was the latter. Since she knew something was off, she may have signed in, but usually they don't give a voluntary admission a "time-based hold." Based on her condition at this point, one could argue it was enough to court order her as "gravely disabled." This means she could not be left alone at any given moment because she cannot, in this state of mind, provide for her own basic personal needs. Thus, it can be argued she could be a danger to herself and gives the court the ability to put a hold on her. Working in the field, I knew this was most likely a minimum. This is in hopes to stabilize the situation but if need be, it will be extended by asking the patient to sign in voluntarily after the hold is up if they are in a better state of mind and are willing to continue treatment. Or the doctor can continue to petition the courts with evidence of treatment with little to no improvement and show the patient needs continued treatment but is unable to make a competent decision for themselves regarding this.

Trying to busy our minds with the next steps and not focus on the worry of Jillian in an unknown psych facility in an enormous city (or the fact that we can't be right there with her), Mother and I begin to gather, sift, and discuss. We talk about the medications related to her symptoms in an attempt to build our own "treatment plan," in hopes to give them something to go off of instead of starting from scratch. I went to Mom's house and went through some folders to read through different lists of medications and notes that were made by Jillian's previous providers from years before. This time, actually having my own understanding of the whole process, I'm ready to jump in and advocate to make this the least traumatic, and hopefully shortest, hospital stay for her.

It wasn't easy to provide help with her care, much to my frustration. In fact, at first, it wasn't even easy to get ahold of someone that would confirm she actually made it to the unit and was safe.

Now, this is completely normal for psych treatment, for the safety of the patients, due to the sensitivity of the situations they find themselves in. I knew this would be the case going in, as I myself have to often use the line, "I cannot confirm nor deny we have a patient here by that name." Knowing this made it no less nerve-wracking. And for those in this same boat, calling to check on someone they care about and being told those words in a robotic, seemingly-uncaring voice is incomprehensible and cold in such an incredibly vulnerable moment.

Once a patient is admitted, they are offered a consent (release of information, aka ROI) to designate who is allowed to know they are there. This consent is often broken down into who can talk to the caregivers about the care being provided and who is able to speak/visit with just the patient themselves. That being said, patients who are admitted for psychosis may take days *or even weeks* before they find themselves in a position to fill this out, especially without prompting. In this situation with Jillian, I was concerned that would most likely be the case.

Unfortunately, in my work experience, even once the patient has filled out the ROI, some co-workers blow off these designated family/friends calling in to check on their loved ones. Yes, at times, they call multiple times a shift for long amounts of time, and at times, inconveniently when we have other things we need to prioritize. But it can make a huge difference to take down the number and give them a call back when there is a moment to provide reassurance. Taking the time to talk with the people who support the patients is vital because the support system they have on the outside is often the biggest resource/factor they have in staying out of our facility and remaining healthy. And in trying to inspire my co-workers to do this, I have told more than one of them about my experience I had when my sister was in California, to remind them just how hard it is to be in that person's shoes and how important it can be to make that person feel heard. That person calling just needs to get a glimpse of hope that the person they care about is even remotely safe and being cared for by someone who goes that extra mile.

I couldn't tell you how many times I called and got the same response:

"We don't have a patient by that name."

Now, this response actually worried me more. Reason being, I say this sometimes when we *really* don't have a patient by that name and the person calling says they have been calling all around and this person they are asking to locate has been missing for x amount of time. We don't have to say the aforementioned 'line' ("I can neither confirm nor deny ... ") to protect the patient with HIPAA in this case because they aren't a patient, so I go the transparent route in hopes they decide to go the welfare check route.

Last I had been able to deduce from Jeff, he had to leave while she was in the ER due to COVID protocols and would not be allowed in-person visits. Imagining the absolute worst-case scenario, as I would, I began to think about that rather cunning sister of mine. Had she "acted" her way out, bounced from the ER, and who knows where she is now? If she is still in the ER, have they fed her or is someone at least checking in on her? Did they give her anything to help her yet, medication to calm her, or at least jumpstart the process to get her mind to slow down?? ERs get busy, and I can't imagine one in LA when even the ones here sometimes have patients sitting for hours, waiting for transfer. They have triaging and traumas galore, forgetting that they also have patients that've been there since before lunch and have yet to eat, and it's now dark outside.

Trying to keep my cool, I was telling myself that not all hospitals are the same, maybe they just don't use the exact same language, she is fine and on the unit.

But I also kept calling because I couldn't keep my cool THAT cool.

They were most definitely ready to block my number if that was a thing hospitals could do.

Finally, at about 11:50 PM Evansville time, I got to talk with a nurse, who at least gave me the time to blurt out, all in one breath,

> "I'm a psych nurse, and I know you can't tell me anything about the patient, I get it, but this is my sister, and I also know you can take down information from me without revealing anything about the patient or breaking HIPAA. I know she was going to be admitted there, her fiancé was with her in the ER and let us know they were placing her on a three-day hold. I just need to know she made it up to you guys from the ER and to try to give you all that I can to help."

He stopped the usual rehearsed responses and began to listen, so I just kept going, hoping that if I say enough words, he'll understand and relent. I further inform him,

> "I just need to leave a message with my name and number to have Jillian call me when she can. I know she is not in the right state of mind to sign consents to say it's okay to let anyone know she is there. Someone is going to have to sit her down and explain to her that, in order for her soon-to-be husband and family to contact her and the hospital, she needs to fill out the paperwork. And I wanted to let you or someone taking

care of her know that I have important information regarding her care, such as medications she has been on in the past and what
worked and didn't."

I was trying not to play the "I'm a nurse" card,
but I couldn't deal any longer with not knowing.
This nurse had compassion. He said she was there
but wasn't able to sign consents at the moment.
Then he suggested to try to call again in the morning to give the information to the treatment team.
So, right before midnight on July 15th, I am able
to let my mom know that she is at least there and
okay. And let out some tears in relief.

Morning of July 16th, I called again. I was
patient and waited until after 10:30 AM (8:30 AM
California time) at least. I again went through part
of the spiel I had the night before, about knowing how HIPAA works and being a psych RN, then
asked the nurse to please go directly ask Jillian for
her permission to speak with me. She seemed an-
noyed, but it worked, I waited on hold and eventually, I got to speak with the unit nurse about Jillian.
Her backstory, what medication she had been on,
her usual disposition, that she has many people in
her support system ready to help.

I can't explain the relief that we might be getting somewhere already. I had to try to make this
go-round better for Jillian, making sure to note that
Risperidone and Paliperidone were NO GO; don't
do it! With psychosis, fairly high doses of Seroquel
worked best and then being weaned off once psychosis had subsided. Then, Lithium was used to

maintain and had been successful. Finally, Jillian had stopped taking medication altogether, as it seemed like there was no need, and she had been okay (even good and thriving) for years, until now.

The nurse then tried to transfer me to Jillian's case manager. This ended up being a never-ending-ringing line. I had to hang up and call the unit back eventually, deciding no one was answering on the other end. I explained the whole thing again and how I was supposed to be transferred to the case manager over her care. The next person I spoke with stated she had not yet been assigned a case manager and would transfer me to the general case manager for the facility. This line also rang ... and rang ... and rang. And it never went to a voicemail, just disconnected.

So, abandoning that for now, I call back to see if I can just talk to my sister. Jillian was confused but also sounded as if she was trying to be positive. I asked if she had any medications yet but she seemed distant and foggy, not answering or even appearing to register the question, mentioning they had just eaten breakfast and casually wondering what Jeff and Kirby were up to out loud. So, I said they were probably at the apartment missing her, and I would have Jeff call her now that I knew we had a better chance to get through.

Later in the evening, I finally got a call back from her case manager that had been assigned and was provided a fax number to send Jillian's previous records. By around 9 PM, Jeff, Mom, and I had all had a chance to speak with Jillian. She sounded downright bubbly, not her usual self and not exactly what one would expect given her current situation. Albeit she was coherent. That was a huge step in the right direction.

Unfortunately, as it goes with psychosis, the path is not often linear. The social worker reported to Jeff that Jillian did not remember why she was there. While we finally had contact, it was still not easy to get ahold of the social worker or nurses caring for Jillian over the next few days. I mostly tried my luck with talking to my sister herself.

This was both cathartic and heartbreaking.

It was so nice to be able to hear Jillian converse and make more sense, but, at the same time, she was pissed. No longer perky, which was somewhat relieving because it seemed a more appropriate reaction, she was now tearful and upset. She felt like mom and I had "put her" there and no one was listening to her, only the people around her. She began to insist that she was fine and wanted to go home. She said over and over that she wished everyone would just stop caring about her because she was fine and didn't need to be in the hospital.

I must admit, I think I am really good at my job with strangers and their feelings, because I can have a sense of detachment and it is healthy. But when it comes to loved ones, I think I struggle with coming off as gentle because of this same sort of seeming detachment. Most who are close to me know I compartmentalize, and showing emotion is not my strong suit, but it is not for lack of caring.

I tried to probe as best I could, with a soft, judgment-free tone. I started by asking her about the concoctions she had been making, and she explained it away as "alchemy." I tried again, asking about her letting Kirby outside without his leash. I was hoping the mention of Kirby and her doing something abnormal with him might jolt her. She instead snapped that there were specific reasons for that, and when I asked her to explain, she said they were reasons for Jeff, not me. Somewhere in the conversation, she also relayed she believed she had ESP. I laid off and tried to change it back to the medical side, the "I'm just a curious nurse," side. I asked if she had any medications, and she said, "Just shots," and could not recall taking anything orally.

Not knowing where else to go with the conversation, I asked her to call me later or tomorrow. She just became more upset with me, saying she didn't want to, as I was being condescending and talking to her like a kid. This part sucked for me, and I teared up, but I also understood where she was coming from. I just wished she could see it from this side because we were all scared. Had any one of the siblings been in her position, I knew she would be just as worried sick.

Some good came from the mostly-not-so-great conversation. She told me she had signed some consents, so I was hoping this meant we would be better able to assist her and get through to staff.

When I did get to talk with the treatment team, I found out that they had not listened to *any* of the advice about medications she had already tried. In fact, it was like they decided they would try **exactly** what we cautioned against, and I was fuming but trying to trust the process at the same time.

Not only did they start Risperidone orally twice a day, but ended up giving her a long-acting injection (LAI) of Paliperidone (Invega Sustenna) before discharge as well. I assume this means they also gave the typical "loading dose" of Invega, but their methods confuse me, so maybe I shouldn't assume anything.

((Just a side note, I found this decision particularly strange to use BOTH medications we suggested they not use. And TOGETHER, as it's usually one or the other, being Paliperidone is a metabolite *of* Risperidone and therefore very similar. For instance, in my experience, an MD might start oral Risperidone to build it up and then switch to the long-acting Risperdal Consta injection, to be given every two weeks. Or they might start with oral Paliperidone and then switch to the long acting Invega injections, for which there are now (as of Sept. 2021) 3 types of FDA-approved strengths, given every 1, 3, or 6 months. At this time, there were 2 types: the 1- and 3-month injections. They gave the 1-month dose (Sustenna). These LAIs can be used alone or in conjunction with Lithium or valproic acid (Depakote) for Bipolar D/O.))

Alas, Jillian left with the Sustenna in her system and scripts to continue the oral Risperdal, Lithium, as well as Remeron when she was discharged the following Tuesday.

And while I was overjoyed she was out, I was holding my breath.

# JEFFREY (HUSBAND)

After I spent some time sitting in the lobby in the wake of Jillian's abrupt departure, an administrative personage came out to ask some questions of me, and—while I did not have written permission from Jillian for them to share everything that was going on—I was her emergency contact, so they had to tell me some things about the process. They informed me she was going to the behavioral unit once a room was prepared and asked what medications she was on, and so on and so forth. But due to the Covid restrictions in place, I could not visit her or see her, and after I was done talking to the admin, she gave me some phone numbers and said to expect some calls later, thus dismissing me; I was not allowed to stay in the waiting room.

So, I wandered around, shoulders slumped, outside of the hospital on a pleasantly warm and sunny LA summer day, with a slight breeze stirring the palm trees, feeling the exact opposite inwardly—utterly bereft, akin to a rudderless ship, lost and alone, after a storm at sea. I immediately began apologizing to Brooke and Jenna, as well as giving updates the best I knew how. I continued wandering around Panorama for a goodly while, at least two or three hours, trying to decompress. I did get a call after a short while informing me that Jillian was being admitted into the behavioral psych ward and that usually patients were given three days until the medical staff reassessed whether someone needed to stay a while longer. The voice on the phone—just another one in the sea of strangers I met and talked to that day—warned me to keep in mind that, since those three days would end on the weekend, I should expect Jillian to stay until at least Monday.

Eventually I made it back to the apartment and helped Kirby vacuum/mop the floors and put away the clothes and kitchen items scattered throughout the apartment. Later that night, I ate a whole stuffed-crust, meat-lovers pizza with Kirby's help. I began very much eating my feelings from that point on. Kirby was initially very happy to see me, but as each day wore on, I could tell he was wondering when his mom would come back.

The next day was frustrating, to say the least. The day before, at the hospital, I was given a couple of different numbers that I could call to check on Jillian; today, I would call and call, and no one was answering. Bewildered, I called the front desk at the hospital. It was explained to me that the number I was calling was the lobby of the psych ward, and the patients were free to answer it, but if the patients didn't want to do so, then I was SOL. Fortunately, Jenna was able to use her "Psych Nurse Card" and wheel and deal her way to get a phone to Jillian. Though Jillian seemed out of it, Jenna was able to convince her to write down names and phone numbers of family members so when she was more cogent, she could make calls. I remember more or less calling the numbers they gave me every hour or two to see if I could get ahold of Jillian. There was one time someone with a very quiet and shy, feminine voice answered the phone and asked who I was. I explained I was trying to get ahold of Jillian Weinzapfel.

"Julian?"

"No JILLIAN, is there a JILLIAN there??"

The quiet voice said, "Oh okay, hold on," and then I waited … and waited … and waited … until I realized that whoever picked up the phone might also be going through some mental health crises, and there would be no Jillian coming to the phone. So, I started yelling "JILLIAN!" through the phone, as I was certain the phone was put down and that—whoever the patient was that answered—she had just aimlessly left and forgot about her mission, but perhaps there was some tiny chance if Jillian was close enough, she would hear a voice shouting at her. I was desperate, but I conceded that perhaps Jillian hearing a disembodied voice calling her name was not the most conducive thing to her current mental health status at this point. It was a fruitless try anyway, as after a goodly five or ten minutes, I finally gave up and ended the call.

It was a disorienting time while Jillian was in the hospital. I had never felt such a complete lack of control over my environment since I could not visit her, and both I and her mom were calling at various times with no luck in getting ahold of anyone. The staff would only confirm that Jillian was there and not, in fact, dead.

Eventually I did get a call from the staff requesting a contact lens case, and I felt like an idiot. I started racking my brain and trying to recall just how long Jillian must have been wearing contacts and never removing them because of her manic condition. I also did not think of sending her with a care package … I had never shipped someone off to a hospital before and wasn't assuming that she would necessarily be gone for a whole week. I had to start asking what kinds of things I could drop off for her (Is it like going to an airport? What kinds of liquids could I drop off? Could I perchance drop off the contact lens solution in addition to the case?). Even the staff I was talking to was not fully aware of what I could bring, but I surmised as long as there were no strings or shoelaces for the patients to hang each other with, it would be okay to give her some sweatpants and a sweatshirt. Although it seemed an unusual thing to pack because it was summer, it occurred to me and made me wonder how cold it might be in those sterilized, freezing hospital rooms with only a little hospital dress to wear.

I put together a tote bag with some clothes I hoped would be acceptable and the contact lens case, of course, as well as some pictures of Jillian and me and some with her family, which I hoped would bring some sort of comfort when she was more aware. I also took it upon myself to pack her favorite book, "The Old Man and the Sea." ... It was not her favorite book, it's actually her least favorite book in the whole world, since Jillian suffers from a mental condition in which she is not capable of liking Ernest Hemingway. Because of this, I also slipped in some other books, just in case. I was not confident she would be able to read them in her current state, but it would be a piece of familiarity and home with her.

Again, it felt odd going to the front of the hospital and waiting outside while a security guard answered through a crack in the door, asking what I needed ... and then simply handing off my tote bag. I could only hope the repeated use of "Jillian Weinzapfel" written all over the care package would be enough to eventually help make its way to her, but I had no idea if it would.

Occasionally I would just wander around the streets near the hospital and frequent the nearby 7-11 for snacks, trying to send positive energy Jillian's way and glancing at my phone to see if maybe I missed any calls from the hospital.

I want to say it was the third day since Jillian was admitted (But at this point the days were all running together.) that she called me. I was a little in shock because I had already called the patient phoneline dozens and dozens of times and was never able to reach her. I do think her mom and sister were able to get ahold of her again and informed me that she seemed clearer than before but was still confused as to why she was in the hospital.

"Hey you!" Jillian said. Her voice was pitched a little bit higher than usual, a bit peppy, but she no longer seemed to be speaking in the manic, euphoric manner that I encountered before her admittance. She still didn't seem to entirely understand why she was in the hospital, but she was chipper and did not seem to be in a bad mood. Only later did I learn just how many drugs they were pumping into her. She related in her chit-chatty way that she wanted to try and help the other patients out while she was there, and that she did get my care bag, and also, she was informed that I had been asking about her. The conversation only lasted a brief while, it seemed, before she had to get ready for bed, as they had a strict "lights out" policy in the psych ward. I was incredibly relieved, though, because she sounded better than she had for a very long time.

The next day, I was still calling the patient phoneline at random times to see if I could get ahold of Jillian, and I still never did. For the dozens upon dozens of times that I called the patient phoneline I never did get ahold of Jillian. Eventually, *she* was able to use the patient phone line to call *me*, once she was in a better state of mind. But, of course, this took a couple of days.

Another endlessly frustrating thing about the Covid policies was that the hospital was only a five-minute walk from the apartment, but I could not go in to see her at any sort of visiting times. There were no visitors allowed whatsoever during the summer of 2020 lockdowns in Southern California. And there was only so much information I could get from the staff, as I did not have a signed medical release form.

Sunday, I received a call from the hospital staff. Because I was Jillian's emergency contact, they needed to make sure I was available and capable of picking her up when they released her. They explained it may be another day or two, yet it was a hopeful sign.

On Tuesday, Jillian was finally released from the hospital. And because of pandemic regulations, I informed the front desk I was there to pick up Jillian by talking to security at the front door, still unable to walk in; I then proceeded to wait outside for two hours or so, even though I was only a half-hour early from the scheduled time.

While I was looking at the front door, Jillian exited at the side door with an attendant, who gave her paperwork and her tote bag; Inside was one of her favorite sweaters that I had packed, which was apparently torn by another patient because they thought it was theirs? It seemed an unlikely explanation since it was a Western Kentucky University sweater, and they most likely had never even traveled to the state of Kentucky.

As we walked back to the apartment, there was an abundance of not completely unexpected cursing, followed by an enraged "If you ever do that to me again I will break up with you." Jillian was relieved to be out of the hospital, but she still seemed to be under the impression that it was a fluke. That she wasn't bipolar. That if I had only been a little more patient with her, she would have been fine. Because there was no way she had a mental health problem. She was fine. And I was a bastard for putting her back in a hospital. I could feel my own anger prickling below the surface—after all, I felt that I'd done everything I could for her, how could she not see that!? But I held my peace as best I could. I didn't think it the time to argue with her; she needed time to process …

HOSPITAL

PANORAMA CITY, CA

PATIENT: WEINZAPFEL, JILLIAN

DISCHARGE SUMMARY

DATE OF ADMISSION: 07/15/2020

DATE OF DISCHARGE: 07/21/2020

IDENTIFICATION: The patient is a 28-year-old Caucasian female, brought in on a 5150 hold for danger to self and gravely disabled.

HISTORY OF PRESENT ILLNESS: The patient was evaluated for hold at ▓▓▓▓▓ ▓▓▓▓▓▓▓ Hospital Emergency Room, brought in by her boyfriend because the patient had not been sleeping, very impulsive, acting bizarre, rambling incoherently, and difficult to redirect. On a face-to-face evaluation, the patient states she had not eating or slept for days. She had poor impulse control, reporting suicidal ideation and unable to contract for safety. The patient was then admitted to reduce risk for self-harm.

HOSPITAL COURSE: She was seen for reality orientation therapy, supportive therapy, and milieu therapy. She is treated with aggressive medication management with Remeron 7.5 mg daily, Risperdal 1 mg twice a day, Depakote 250 twice a day, and Invega Sustenna 234 mg was given and a booster dose 156 mg also given.

OUTCOME: The patient had better coping skills. Denying suicidal ideation. Denies feeling hopeless and helpless. Contracted for safety.

MENTAL STATUS EXAMINATION:
APPEARANCE: She appears stated age. Fair hygiene.
BEHAVIOR: Cooperative.
MOOD: Appropriate.
AFFECT: Constricted.
THOUGHT PROCESS: Linear.
THOUGHT CONTENT: The patient denies suicidal ideation and contracted for safety.

DISCHARGE DIAGNOSIS: BIPOLAR AFFECTIVE DISORDER, DEPRESSED TYPE.

*Discharge paperwork from my first stay at the hospital in Panorama City. Note the laundry list of medications and that sweet diagnosis. (2020)*

HOSPITAL
Medication Reconciliation Order Form

Use for: ☐ Transfer
☑ Discharge

Patient Name: WEINZAPFEL, JILLIAN V.

Visit ID:

Admitted: 07/15/2020

Location: PSYCH UNIT SOUTH

MR Number:

Attending:

Admitting Diagnosis:

DOB:

| Allergies | | Allergy Date |
|---|---|---|

No Known Allergies
TYPE: Drug Allergy

| Inpatient Medications | | |
|---|---|---|
| Drug | Order Start Date | Continue Medication Yes No |
| HydrOXYzine Pamoate (VISTARIL) 50 MG CAPSULE<br>VISTARIL<br>50 MG ORAL EVERY 6 HOURS AS NEEDED<br>Instructions:<br>CPOE COMMENT: ANXIETY/AGITATION<br>NOT TO EXCEED 200MG/24HOURS | 07/15/2020 23:07 | ☐ ☐ |
| ACETAMINOPHEN 325MG (TYLENOL) 325 MG TABLET<br>TYLENOL<br>650 MG ORAL EVERY 4 HOURS AS NEEDED<br>Instructions:<br>CPOE COMMENT: MILD PAIN (PAIN SCALE 1-3)<br>TEMPERATURE GREATER THAN 100<br>*TYLENOL NOT TO EXCEED 3 GRAMS IN 24 HOURS FROM ALL SOURCES* | 07/15/2020 23:07 | ☐ ☐ |
| ALUM-MAG HYDROXIDE-SIMETH (MYLANTA) 200-200-20 MG/5 ML SUSPENSION<br>MYLANTA<br>30 ML ORAL EVERY 4 HOURS AS NEEDED<br>Instructions:<br>CPOE COMMENT: GI DISCOMFORT OR HEARTBURN | 07/15/2020 23:07 | ☐ ☐ |
| TRAZODONE (OESYREL) 50 MG TABLET<br>DESYREL<br>50 MG ORAL AT BEDTIME AS NEEDED<br>Instructions:<br>CPOE COMMENT: INSOMNIA X 15 DAYS<br>MAY REPEAT X 1 | 07/15/2020 23:07 | ☐ ☐ |
| MIRTAZAPINE (REMERON) 15 MG TABLET<br>REMERON<br>7.5 MG ORAL AT BEDTIME | 07/16/2020 21:00 | ☑ ☐ |
| RISPERIDONE (RISPERDAL) 1 MG TABLET<br>RISPERDAL<br>1 MG ORAL TWICE A DAY<br>Instructions: CAUTION: HAZARDOUS DRUG<br>OBSERVE SPECIAL HANDLING, ADMINISTRATION AND DISPOSAL REQUIREMENTS. | 07/16/2020 10:00 | ☑ ☐ |

HOSPITAL
Medication Reconciliation Order Form

Use for: ☐ Transfer
☐ Discharge

Patient Name: WEINZAPFEL, JILLIAN V.

Visit ID:

Admitted: 07/15/2020

Location: PSYCH UNIT SOUTH

MR Number:

Attending:

Admitting Diagnosis:

DOB:

| Inpatient Medications | | |
|---|---|---|
| Drug | Order Start Date | Continue Medication Yes No |
| LITHIUM CARB CAP (LITHOBID) 300 MG CAPSULE<br>LITHOBID<br>300 MG ORAL TWICE A DAY | 07/17/2020 09:00 | ☑ ☐ |
| PALIPERIDONE PALMITATE 234 MG/1.5 ML SYRINGE<br>INVEGA SUSTENNA<br>117 MG/0.75 ML IM EVERY MONTH | 07/21/2020 09:00 | ☑ ☐ |

*The Medication Reconciliation Order Form from my first stay at the Panorama City Hospital. (2020)*

# CHAPTER TWELVE

I was in the hospital for … I don't know how many days. My memory around my California hospitalizations is considerably foggier than those in Indiana, and that's saying something.

A result of it still being too soon to revisit them? Or was I far enough gone that I have no memories to return to?

I honestly don't know.

But I left understandably shaken. And humiliated once again.

Jeff helped me piece together the damage I'd done before being admitted to the hospital. Our apartment was torn asunder. I had posts galore online that were vague, disconcerting, bewildering quips. And direct message conversations that were, in a word, mortifying. More friendships just *POOF!* gone for good. I miraculously only spent $100 through this episode. Somehow I managed to put a cap on it, though, how, I couldn't even begin to say.

At least I didn't ruin us financially.

Not at first.

With more time to dedicate to a search, Jeff picked up where he left off in finding me a psychiatrist. We found Dr. M _ _ _ , and she was wonderful. I began also talking to a therapist named Karen. Between the two of them, a swift $120 was being drained from our bank account weekly.

Perhaps that wouldn't have done too much fiscal damage on its own, but I wanted to go ahead with our wedding ceremony and make it a more private, less stress-inducing affair. The wedding planning I was supposed to be doing was an impossible task looming on the horizon, causing panic and anxiety that I wasn't capable of handling, all things considered.

I found a local couple that hosted weddings on their own property, a lovely venue in Agoura Hills. The husband officiated the weddings, and his wife notarized the paperwork, ran the music, and filmed/photographed the events. The entire shindig would cost ~$650, a far cry from what the full-scale wedding and reception back home would amount to.

It was perfect. We cancelled our Indiana venue, reset our wedding date for August 20, 2020, and made plans to cement our union sooner.

I was on a slew of medications … I'd have to look back at my records to know precisely which ones. My first meeting with Dr. M _ _ _ was frustrating for both of us. She couldn't even diagnose me, I was such a drooly, shaky mess. She was unable to decipher anything I was saying and proceeding with treatment looked dubious.

In the meantime, she determined we needed to taper off the antipsychotics I had coursing through my body. She could at least discern I was on far too many.

This was reinforced by the frustrations I experienced in trying to complete basic, day-to-day tasks. I could barely dress myself. Everything was numb. I couldn't lift my arms over my head. Jeff had to help me bathe, brush my hair, brush my teeth. I was useless, practically a vegetable.

I wasn't able to return to nannying as I had hoped I would, so Jeff helped me reach out to the Halaris family and tell them what was going on.

It truly broke my heart. I loved those kids.

Jeff tried to help my life seem as normal as he could. I remember him suggesting a trip to the beach.

The drive there was painful. My legs were bouncing constantly and the pain at not extending them fully was excruciating. And the heat was unbearable. The temperatures had climbed to the 120°F zone.

Masks were now mandated, and even the beach crowds donned face coverings.

Mine was drenched in drool. I was unable to breathe in my mask, and the lack of oxygen resulted in uncontrollable saliva.

And forget walking. Jeff would be strolling at a leisurely pace, and it took everything I had to keep up with him. My legs wouldn't move properly.

Brain and body broken, I was very slow to recuperate.

Upon discussing our mutual distaste for Lithium, Dr. M _ _ _ prescribed Lamictal, and Jeff and I miraculously managed to pick it up at the pharmacy. It was no easy feat.

Initially, the day the Lamictal was supposed to be ready to pick up at the pharmacy, it was nowhere to be found. And so began the furious race to alert Dr. M _ _ _ .

In order to reach her, our calls were routed through an indirect answering service. Sometimes the calls were disconnected. Sometimes they couldn't understand what I was saying through all the drooling and slurring of words, and Jeff had to take over. Sometimes the messages we *finally* left successfully still didn't reach Dr. M _ _ _ .

Unfortunately, we'd run into so many problems trying to get ahold of the medication that by the time we finally were able to obtain it, the mania had reared its ugly head and was taking back over.

Here we go again.

# JEFFREY (HUSBAND)

Upon our arrival to our apartment, Kirby was overjoyed to see and have 'Mom' back. Between Jillian and me, though, there was a great deal of tension and awkwardness. She was fine, completely fine, and there was never any cause for her to go to the hospital. Maybe her "OCD" had flared up, but that was no reason to be imprisoned in the psych ward. Her mood grew substantially worse over the next couple of days due to all of the meds—she was taking at least four separate drugs—in addition to the ongoing reaction to the shot of Invega they administered right before releasing her, which had a cumulative and severe effect on her motor skills. She was thinking clearly, if cynically, and in total denial about her recent behaviour. This denial was not coming from the manic, dream state, unattached-to-reality episode she was previously in. Rather, this was old-fashioned, normal, highly-typical denial coming from a place of fear. Fear that she was, in fact, bipolar.

It wasn't long before her attention was needed elsewhere because suddenly moving was getting harder for her. Within a couple of days she was moving like a stroke victim. She couldn't walk quickly (much less at a normal pace), had trouble grasping things, her speech was slurred, and she drooled unless she was making a concerted effort not to.

She was supposed to have a scheduled outpatient session with a psychiatrist the hospital referred her to, but—as I'd already managed to find Doctor M___'s office before her hospitalization even took place—we stuck to the original plan. Besides, Jillian didn't feel she could trust anyone the hospital would refer her to anyway, so this was her best bet. In their first appointment, conducted via Telehealth (video conferencing, as was the Covid protocol), Dr. M___ felt she was unable to even begin to diagnose Jillian because she was so heavily-medicated that Dr. M___ couldn't see what was going on in her voice or face. And, of course, because the doctor was unable to meet with her in person to gather clues from any further body language, she was at a complete loss. Dr. M___ tried to wean Jillian off of most of her drugs except for Lithium, and she was very irritated and frustrated they drugged Jillian up to such a degree.

There was still a cumulative effect of taking all these drugs in addition to the Invega shot; the effects of this drug alone were supposed to last for an entire month, so there was no way to wean off of it except to wait. I always suspected the Invega was the primary driver of her poor motor skills, but of course it would be difficult to say given the entire slew of medications she was prescribed upon discharge.

Jillian had to really work to coordinate our rescheduled wedding to a new venue that was a short drive out of LA in idyllic Agoura Hills. It was such a struggle for her to speak on the phone, and she could not keep herself from slurring. The woman who would eventually host our wedding was thankfully very patient, kind, and understanding as Jillian tried to explain why she was having such a hard time speaking. We were, of course, hoping the side effects from the drugs would abate enough by early August, in plenty of time to be married on the 20th.

At one point we went to the beach to try and relax and destress from the overwhelming intensity of the last few weeks. I drove, of course, since Jillian could not handle the pedals … or the steering wheel … or really, any of the car, for that matter. Her coordination, her motor skills, everything was rendered inadequate for her. When we made it to our favorite beach, I took off at a normal pace through the sand to find a good spot to put down our towels, and when I looked back, to my chagrin, Jillian was far-off, hobbling and trying to get my attention, as she could not keep up, and she was really trying, and out of breath, and very distraught that I did not notice sooner. Once we were settled, she was unable to relax comfortably, she was having trouble breathing (*especially* with her face mask, as was the current Covid protocol), and we ended up calling the beach picnic short.

Throughout the days since she'd been released, Jillian was still searching for some other reason why these mental health episodes occurred, something other than the humiliating term "bipolar". She embraced that Dr. M___ could not diagnose her as evidence that she was, for the most part, fine. It was just sensory overload.

Gradually, albeit at a much slower pace than either of us preferred, Jillian's movement and speech began improving. The shot of Invega was supposed to wear off after a month, and—after around three weeks—she finally started moving better. Her next appointment with Dr. M___ seemed more successful, and she was prescribed a different medication, Lamotrigine (aka Lamictal), which was intended to circumvent the side effects she was getting from all the other meds, and which Dr. M___ far-preferred to Lithium. I know the doctor was unconvinced Jillian did not have bipolar disorder and was withholding an official diagnosis until she was without any doubt, but Jillian took the lack of a diagnosis as a sign that she was fine and even started embracing that she instead had "Synesthesia." She was just highly sensitive to music and sound, and this must be what kicked her brain into overdrive. Walt Disney is purported to have "synesthesia," so she must have been in good company. She was still grasping at any straw available to her, and who could blame her? Though I tried not to humor her too much, I understood the impulse.

Dr. M___ was set to go on a brief vacation to visit with her son. She congratulated Jillian and me on our soon-to-be wedding and told us the next appointment would be in three weeks.

This extended window of time turned out to be disastrous.

It became clearer and clearer that Jillian's mania was still bubbling just below the surface, waiting to be unleashed once again. She practically swung the door wide open for it. Once Dr. M___ expressed the same disdain for Lithium and prescribed her Lamictal, Jillian—without express permission from the psychiatrist—immediately stopped the Lithium. She felt great now that the medications' side effects from the hospital were fading. In fact, she felt really great—more herself than ever before—and if the whole world would simply recognize the beauty and harmony and interconnectedness of everything then wow, what an incredible thing that would be, and it's just so frustrating and dumb that people don't realize the circle of life and it makes her so angry now. Her mood swings were once again giving me emotional whiplash.

Unfortunately, that was not the only hole to plug in our sinking ship. We had a difficult time obtaining the Lamictal, and not for lack of trying. The prescription order was sent to a random Walgreens Pharmacy in New Mexico; we never were able to figure out why or how that happened. There was a whole back-and-forth in which we were forced to convince the pharmacy to fill out the same prescription in LA. Once we finally obtained the Lamictal, Jillian only took a few of the pills she was supposed to take. She cited concerns about uncontrollable heart palpitations that frightened her. Additionally, since Jillian felt she had synesthesia and not any other medical condition, she decided to stop taking it altogether, as well as any and all other medications.

Jillian's mother convinced her to at least let the doctor know she stopped taking her medications, and I was relieved for that. With fresh energy, released from the burden of taking medication, her moods began swinging back and forth from elation and wonder about the world, to a dark rage. For instance, there was once that—after I convinced her to take *half* a Lamictal tablet if she wasn't going to take a full one, for me, as a favor—she laid down for ten seconds, then sprung up lashing out at how everyone is against her, and all her family "doesn't get it," and "*no one* gets it," and 'they' need to wake up etc., etc., etc. The moods were unpredictable, and I never knew where they might be coming from or going. I continued my default mode of accepting whatever it was Jillian ended up monologuing about and tried to ask questions and gently probe if some of the things she was doing were not the most practical. She signed up to a lot of auditions and an acting subscription list, as it felt some of these opportunities she saw online were just so *her* and fit her to a T. It was obvious to me, and to her family, that she had still not fully recovered, and now—with the absence of medication—her mania was making a ferocious comeback.

It seemed to happen even quicker than before.

She stopped sleeping, and I couldn't even recall the last time she had a full night's sleep anyway, due to her physical discomfort on the medications (She was always waking up and suffering from terrible spasms and tremors in her hands at all hours. And they weren't small, fidgety spasms, but spasms that would have her entire arms gesticulating out of her control. And there was continual drooling when she wasn't concentrating and forcing herself not to, making it difficult for her to breathe.). Her mother and siblings began messaging me in earnest; they could sense it too. There was, once again, a round of back-and-forth on the phone trying to get some medical professional to see Jillian. I started with calling Dr. M___'s office, but the actual "front desk" was an outsourced company based in Asia (I think it might have been in the Philippines … I forget now exactly where my call was being routed to, but it was not in the US, according to the people who were answering the phones.). I desperately tried to reinforce the urgency with which I was calling and begged they pass along the message that I was Jillian's fiancé, I was living with her, and Jillian had stopped taking her medication. I understood that Dr. M___ was on a vacation, but if she could check in … or perhaps we could quickly get an appointment with someone else scheduled in? I was promised by more than one person that the message would be relayed, and I thought surely they would get back to me soon.

Jillian started dressing herself in layers and layers of clothes and kept on being creative with the objects around her: She was moving around her plants, adding spices and other objects into the pots in order to garner some sort of positive growth energy? I stashed all of our extra cash and valuables into an alcove tucked away in the side closet where I knew she would never think to look, as well as all of the knives and sharp objects I could find.

It was a Friday, I had a shift to work at the gas station, and I kept going back and forth in my mind on whether or not I could leave Jillian alone. After all, she seemed mentally just fine only a short, couple of days ago. The window for me to call off of work was quickly closing. I eventually decided that, because it was not a busy gas station, and I was alone there for most of the night to close up, I might as well take her with me, so long as she promised that she would sit in the corner and not wander off. Fortunately, the owner happened to be there auditing the cash in the store and saw Jillian. The owner, Roda (my boss), was a middle-aged woman from Jordan in the Middle East, who always thought of me as one of her best workers. Seeing Jillian and the absent-minded, unintelligible way she was speaking (Once again, she was speaking articulately, if not logically, to me just moments before, but—suddenly in public—she started using motions and sign language.), the owner thought two things: A) Jillian was beautiful and B) Yes, something was the matter with her, and she clearly wasn't acting normally. I explained, without delving into dark details, that she had been on medication, but it was recently switched, and her brain is reeling and having some sort of reaction because she is obviously not herself, and I was afraid to leave her alone. Roda was completely sympathetic, allowed us to grab some water and a snack for Jillian—free of charge—and told me not to worry about my shift tonight or tomorrow, that she would find someone to cover.

While I was driving us back to the apartment, Jillian kept stuffing more and more items and trash into the glove compartment until it couldn't close, but she kept at it. She fielded calls from her family checking in with her, and, once again, she could speak in surprisingly articulate English, though it was still abundantly clear she was detached from reality. She decided to text the employers she was nannying for that she needed a vacation. This, of course, was very odd for them to hear, as they knew she had been to the hospital but were unaware of just how bad her condition was, and they had graciously been letting her stay at home and not come into work for an entire month by this point. I tried to stop her and distract her from texting them, but—not only was I too late—I was driving, so I did not think it wise to try and snatch the phone from her hand. I was already despairingly struggling to make her keep her seatbelt on, as she was repeatedly unbuckling it and moving about, exploring the car.

I got a call from the father of the children Jillian nannied for. Previously, I notified both parents, after admitting her, that she would not make it to work, and she was all right— that it wasn't Covid-related—but I was purposely vague, as I didn't want to endanger her employment. It was her story to tell, not mine, if she decided to share it. Jillian had also briefly spoken to them on the phone after the hospital, and, due to the slurring, they could tell she was not well. Now, on this particular call, while I was still somewhat sugarcoating the severity of just how insensible she was at times, I also felt compelled to be more forthright and painted the picture that—from my end—she only had about four hours of sleep, in total, the week before she went to the hospital, and it felt like she was sleepwalking while simultaneously not being able to fully sleep. I explained the hospital then pumped her full of an absurd amount of meds, and—as her psychiatrist switched what meds she was on—she went back to a state of not sleeping, and her brain just kind of stopped, because she's right back to just not getting any sleep. It was the best I knew how to describe her current circumstances without being disingenuous. I did not want to share the buzzwords "manic" or "bipolar." Yet, the father had friends that had gone through their own mental health crises, and he seemed very understanding and sympathetic. Jillian had watched over their kids for almost two years, and they never sensed anything unreasonable or off about her and trusted her fully with their children. They were understandably confused and concerned when she texted she needed a vacation after being so consistently dependable and hard-working.

I again held onto false hope that the psychiatrist's office would get back to me, and I called them one more time with a warning that—if I didn't get an immediate phone call from a doctor—I would have to take Jillian back to the hospital.

It was a very long night.

I was as alert as I could be to whatever creative enterprises she was attempting and tried my best to mitigate them. I was constantly turning the stoves and oven off while she was making her concoctions; she was grabbing anything she could get her hands on in the kitchen to mix together. Even Kirby sensed Jillian was off and was therefore hiding in the bedroom, too alarmed to come out.

Within what felt like a handful of minutes (and simultaneously a hundred years), she had clogged the toilet with a whole onion and doggy bags, the bathroom sink with plants and condiments she poured out, and the bathtub with clothes and various items found throughout the apartment. I kept heading her off and putting things back before they got wet. and asked her to stop, while beseeching her to take some Lithium, which she agreed to and acted like she was going to do, but—to my dismay—spit it out. Granted, I doubt it would have helped at this point, but I didn't want to send her back to the hospital. She would never forgive me if she had to go back, and perhaps if she took some of her medication, it would take the edge off her mental health crisis, pull the rug out from under its metaphorical feet, even if just barely halting the speed at which it was destroying her again.

Not losing any steam, Jillian kept putting all of these clothes on—layers upon layers—and mentioned that she was leaving to go home. To try and clear up my confusion (since, as far as I knew, we *were* home), I tried questioning her as to where she thought home was. She threw out her catch phrase again, saying, "It's a long story, but you know where home is, and that's where we should go." She had travel bags packed full of the most random junk, in preparation of her leaving. I continued asking her questions in order to distract her from leaving the apartment. After about an hour or two, she put her bags down and with a great sigh said, "Phew, I'm glad to be home." Because in her mind she had gone through the journey already? I had no idea, and I knew she wouldn't be able to explain beyond it being a "long story." At least she was no longer planning on leaving the apartment.

For the briefest of moments when she seemed to slow down, I knew she was texting Jenna, and I peeked at her phone when she happened to be sitting, and her head repeatedly began to dip, and she seemed to close her eyes and be still. Out of sheer curiosity, I just had to know what in the world her messages might look like. I only saw a message or two, but they went along the lines of her sister saying,

"You should get some sleep girl!"

Jillian's reply?

"Oh I have been trying to."

I remembered thinking you would have no idea how distorted her mind was at this moment by her texting; she could spit out general platitudes very well. Also, try and imagine my shock in seeing "I have been trying to [sleep]." Oh, she has been trying to??!??! The HECK she had been. Every chance I could, I tried coaxing her into laying down and resting, hoping that she would actually find real sleep, yet she was always refusing. ALWAYS. She'd lay down, and her head-resting only lasted a moment before she was back up at it, ready to make some more interesting cocktails with whatever she could find in the kitchen.

There was one point when I truly reached my peak: She kept putting clothes in the bathtub, and out of my exhaustion—for the first time in weeks, as far as I could remember—I finally snapped and lost my cool. I kept telling her not to put clothes into the bathtub, which was full of water and also clogged. I would snatch the clothes and put them back in the closet, but then she'd find others and continue putting them in the tub. I grabbed her by the shoulders and, shaking her, yelled, "Would you fucking stop!?" She froze up for half a minute ... and then she went back to putting clothes in the bathtub. To my shame, this is one of the only things Jillian seems to recall in the days leading up to her second hospital stay: me grabbing her. It so shocked her, and it still did absolutely nothing. A mere half-minute where she stopped moving, and then she went about in her own dream-world like nothing happened. I was exhausted and in retrospect I should have taken her in the dead of night to the ER right then (if not much sooner), but I felt these were the last moments I had with Jillian as a couple, and I was hanging on by a thread in more ways than one.

She was collecting dirt, gum, and jewelry to add into her flowerpot at 2 AM, and I slumped into the corner chair and put my head in my hands. I resigned myself that once I escorted her back to the hospital, she would probably call off our engagement, especially considering the entire month-plus—whether in mid-episode or not—she was convinced there was nothing wrong with her. I did not think we would last as a couple, given the hostility and hurt she felt I was the cause of: forcing her into the hospital, manipulating her to take prescription drugs she didn't feel she needed, etc.

But I didn't know what else to do. I couldn't take care of her anymore.

Jillian was puttering around the kitchen again when I gave up cleaning after her and instead moped into the bedroom and laid down on the bed, for just a moment. I was so tired and rather morose about our future by now, but I softly petted Kirby as he was very anxious and confused by the dynamic he sensed. I closed my eyes … and went to sleep.

I woke up in a horrified panic and was immediately relieved to hear Jillian still in the kitchen doing who-knows-what and making quite the racket. Thankfully she had been engaged with what was in front of her. I still shudder to think what would have happened if she had decided to "travel home," again while I was asleep. I was only out for an hour, and when I walked back into the main room of our apartment, Jillian was holding our largest knife, idly scratching the front door. She also had a special drink that was "reeeally good," if I wanted to try some. I saw all the flour, sugar, gum, empty cans lying around and in this big cup was this mash of yuck that she must have at least sipped.

I declined …

# **JENNA** (YOUNGER SISTER/ PSYCH NURSE)

Now, we wait. And watch.

Of course, watching from halfway across the nation is as easy as it sounds.

I was relying on updates from Jillian, who was obviously less-than-thrilled about her new drug regimen and very determined to find any OTHER diagnosis she could. I was watching social media, somewhat in fear of what she may post, but hoping to catch a glimpse of her to determine my own opinion. And I was waiting on updates from Jeff. This one was tricky, as I was trying my best not to bother him due to the immense amount of dealings he was undergoing already. So, my choices were either wait to hear it directly from him or maybe get something passed on from my mother.

Now, don't get me wrong, I cherished the fact that I could communicate with Jillian so readily through our personal lines and not have to go through the hospital spiderweb of a phone net-work anymore. The task at hand was the balance between trying to be there for her and listen, as a sister, without throwing in my two cents as a nurse. This became especially difficult when she began to directly talk about medications, diagnoses, side effects, and the like. On the one hand, it's an open invitation for me to use my knowledge and try to help from the nurse perspective, right? But, on the other hand, she also is NOT in the mindset to listen to medical professionals at this point in time because she is still not accepting the fact that "bi-polar" fits. So, it is like walking through a minefield, trying to gently assert my belief but also not push it on her because she's my sister and I don't want her to stop talking to me. I don't want to alienate myself or make myself seem like a "traitor" to her, because then what good will I be?

Thus, our conversations were somewhat lack-ing. Speaking with Jillian at this time was, in the nicest way possible, a task.

## Exhibit A.
August 5th, she let me know she was off the Lithium.

Inside, I am panicking. Through text, I reply, "Yay!!!"

But silver linings were there. She was in a good mood, her motor skills were improving although not totally there (she described them as "shit" still), and she was going to try to go jog with Jeff the next day. She was also seeing an outpatient doctor and seemed to have good rapport with this one already. That was promising! She wasn't going to be off medication completely; they were going to begin Lamictal. She asked me what I knew about this one, so I told her what I knew from my experience: It seemed to be a good one, as many of my patients that used Lamictal for bipolar seemed to be pretty "with it." It also seemed to be not such a heavy hitter and was also used for seizure disorder. We both mentioned feeling hopeful about this one, pending any weird reactions.

She did say something that worried me at this point though:

> "Worse comes to worst I can go back on Celexa. That one worked for a WHILE."

Trying my best not to let myself get into it, I simply replied,

> "I think Lamictal will be the one, I have a good feeling lol."

Meanwhile, my brain is screaming, "NO MA'AM YOU CANNOT GO BACK ON CELEXA. HELLO, DO YOU NOT REMEMBER THE FIRST EPISODE AND HOW WE GOT HERE???" I change the subject to myself to distract her and say I don't feel good. Give her something to discuss besides her own ailments. It works for the moment.

**Exhibit B.**
August 6th, she texts me around 3:30 AM and says she is back to not being able to sleep at the moment. Shit. I was asleep though, and when I replied the next day, she said she actually did fall asleep and slept until 9, so I let the worry go. Just

a fluke. Sometimes people can't sleep. It's fine, everything is fine.

When I mentioned a couple moments ago that I didn't feel well, it wasn't JUST a distraction technique. I really didn't, but I didn't think it would be anything to note. Until I'm down and out with COVID a couple days later and all I have to do to pass time is play on my phone or sleep. So, Jillian and I spend a lot of time the next week or so talking, either on Facetime or texting. This is where it began to get a little harder to tote the line between sister and nurse, as she began to delve deeper into finding a different cause to explain what was going on with her.

**Exhibit C.**
August 10th, she lets me know that she will not be taking her medication tonight. Earlier that day, she had debated taking half a dose of the Lamictal, but had since decided against this and said she wanted me to hear it from her. She also sends me articles about "Fantasia is Disney Brand Symphonic Synesthesia" and "Sensory Links between Autism and Synesthesia," stating "I think this may be what I have." So, here begins more of the balancing act. I am trying not to push it, in hopes I wouldn't make her more set on not taking any of it, but I also have to figure out what she is thinking. She says her "findings" about Synesthesia made her decide against the half-dose, but worse than that, she echoes that she thinks Celexa was right for her.

I know better than to straight argue with what she is saying and I have to admit, what the articles talk about does seem similar to how some people with bipolar d/o describe the sensory feelings. I can see where she may feel the connection, and who am I to disregard that, never having experienced it?

I tell her that while the articles may fit, I don't think it is the whole picture and I still think she should try half a dose. I hope just dismissing the comment about Celexa will work. She agrees that it isn't the full picture either, which is great, but still isn't mentioning bipolar d/o. Instead, it's depression, anxiety, PTSD, OCD. All could be relevant, sure, but from what we have all witnessed to this point from the outside looking in, I just don't feel it's enough to cover what she has displayed. I focus on the medicine, again saying,

> "Which the Lamictal might help with, I think try the half dose and see how that makes you feel."

All I get back to that is, "Ok."

I backtrack a bit (wimpy, I know), again, trying to make sure I am maintaining my sister role and not overstepping my bounds here. I say "but obviously it's up to you. When do you talk to the psychiatrist next?" She mentions she is trying to call the office now, but the doctor is on vacation, then sends me another article on synesthesia.

I wait for a bit, to give her some space and try to make it feel like I am not hounding her, even though that is exactly what I am doing. I ask what her plan is. She says,

"Not sure. Probably not take the meds. See how I do."

Damn.

**Exhibit ... D? Is that where we're at?**
August 11th, Jillian texts me saying,

"Mom's mad at me now. Because I'm bring-ing genetics into the conversation."

Now, at this lovely time of COVID quarantine for me, I am actually unable to quarantine at my own (new) home due to work being done and not wanting to infect said workers. So, I am at my mother's to quarantine and have already heard from my mother that Jillian is mad at her. Great place to be, in the middle, isn't it? I try my best to ease into this, saying maybe it was miscommunica-tion, as Mom thought Jillian might be upset with her. Jillian says she is not mad either.

Jillian then sends me the screenshot of what she sent Mom:

"This is what I'm talking about. You assume I'm mentally ill and not just differently abled. I think our whole family is differently abled in a way that sets us apart from "normal" people. We're full of joy. Does it stress us out sometimes? Of course it does, Other people love to hate on happy people. But we're stubborn about it. We're going to be happy, dammit. I think we all have the music and dance in us. I just have it at a stronger level than I can sometimes handle. There's no denial. You and dad gave me my love for music and dance. So yes, it's all your faults (winky emoji). I'm proud of who I am."

After this, Jillian states, "She hung up on me." Jillian believes Mom hung up because she brought up restless leg syndrome. I tell her that Mom didn't mention a single word about that, so I don't think that is it. So, Jillian comes to the conclusion that Mom isn't listening then. She feels Mom wants it to be Jillian's "problem" but says it isn't a problem for her to be different, she always has been. Then, AGAIN with the Celexa. She says,

> "I still think the Celexa would help for a bit, but ultimately I need to look at amino acid levels. I need to eat more blueberries, Lol."

I am losing the battle as the sister now. It isn't working, so with not much else to lose, I'm ready to give the nurse in me a go. My frustration is at an all-time high, but I am still trying to maintain a therapeutic manner. I try to explain how I see it and how I believe my mom sees it. I tell Jillian that she keeps talking about "diagnoses" and Mom has tried to tell her she isn't concerned with what diagnosis is given. Ultimately, Mom wants Jillian to give the medication a fair chance to work, especially since she has a psychiatrist appointment in a week and won't have anything to report on if she hasn't been taking the medication she is supposed to. Jillian claims she told her doctor she isn't taking the medication, so I ask what the doctor had to say about this? Well, Jillian hasn't been able to tell her directly still as she is still on vacation. So, from my understanding, the doctor is unaware at this point. Jillian says,

"Maybe.

But it isn't a mood disorder.

My mood is stable af."

I want to scream. Instead, I reply that Mom and I both feel she should at least give half a dose of the Lamictal a chance each day until she talks with the doctor next. Just to see how it is. Then, in another attempt to ease the whole diagnosis obsession, I reiterate that no one is saying it is a mood thing but the medication is what the doctor, who has years of schooling and experience, believes would help.

Trying to further explain how "stable af" her mood is, she says she is, "Listening to chill beats and doing dishes and cleaning," at the moment. And, to counter my point that no one is claiming it is a mood disorder, "Mom is saying it's a mood thing." Jillian says, "She still believes it's bipolar. She won't step away from that ledge."

Jillian and I discuss a bit further and she does admit,

"I'm not denying there's a chemical imbalance."

I am hoping this is an "in," so I say,

"Then why don't you take the medication for the chemical imbalance?"

Jillian sticks to her stance that it is not the one for her, "I already know, I'm OCD, I know my body. I did try it."

I lose all therapeutic tone here. My blood boils. I'm sorry, even re-reading the texts today as I type this narrative, I want to throw my phone across the room.

"I DID TRY IT" ?!?!?!?!

I reply,

"You took one dose Jillian. Don't be dumb."

"Yep."

DEEP BREATH.

"You know that's not how it works."

"I'm not being dumb. I'm being super smart."

I cannot believe she is being this dense. This is not Jillian. I simply state I disagree. She sends back a few texts, one that says agree to disagree and another with a gif of Donald Trump and her added caption of "Smartest person alive" then another with "LMAO" and "I'm sorry, I'm just messing with you at this point," but I am just done with the conversation for now.

She tries to Facetime me, but I make excuses that I don't feel like it, and I am busy doing other things on my phone. She says I am mad at her and I don't want her to think this. While our previous texts upset me, I can't be mad at her right now. She has enough on her own plate without me adding to the stress. I tell her she will be paused the whole time, still trying to get out of Facetime, but she says she doesn't mind. Running out of excuses, we Facetime.

I can't exactly remember the finer details of our Facetime, but judging by the texts sent afterwards, it was not a great conversation. This is the first time in our texts that I show true anger towards her in months. From what I can gather, I felt that she put words in my mouth, as the first text I sent after ending the call was,

> "Don't put fucking words in my mouth, 'oh you don't trust me cause you think I have mental illness,' that's fucking bullshit."

Astute observation, I know.

Okay, so reading through the other texts, I further gather that we began to discuss more research that Jillian found relevant to her case. She also sent me a picture of a pill bottle of N-A-C Sustain. This being N-Acetyl-L-Cysteine, an antioxidant amino acid, which according to the picture she sent, supports liver and lung function. I assume I called into question something to do with her research of another explanation/treatment plan, or again mentioned it may not be the full picture, as I was always treading lightly. She may have become offended and defensive, calling my trust into question but also bringing in the factor of it being due to my belief of her having a mental illness. Thus, I became offended, because my whole career is working with the mentally ill, and I become overly-sensitive to stigmatizing those with mental illness as incapable of intelligence. In fact, I will be the first to tell you I believe those who suffer from mental illness (especially with psychotic brands) are usually of abnormally-high intelligence in my experience.

So, I am angry. And I inform Jillian of this, stating that the reason her research isn't the ONLY research I am willing to trust is because of that stigma that she is displaying every time she herself talks about mental illness because she doesn't want to have a mental illness. Which is fine (who would?), but then she can't say she isn't biased in her own research. And to my surprise, she apologizes. She says she is not upset with me and she is sorry she made me angry. I'm still a bit fired up, but less so, yet I want to drive home my point. So, I say,

> "You make me angry because you keep placing stigmas on mental illness when like every fucking person on the planet has one."

And finally, I think we may be getting some-where. Maybe anger needed to be shown, because now it seems we are having a real con-versation.

She doesn't think, feel, or believe this is what she is doing. Which, of course I don't believe was ever her intention to do either. I know she is trying to figure out her own self, not the rest of the world and its issues.

Then she says, "I'm just… weird."

Yeah, no shit. (Just kidding, kind of.)

She then points out,

> "You know what it's like when everyone around you wants to diagnose YOU, with alcoholism for example. It's infuriating to hear other people assess you without your input. That's how I feel."

I try again to get across to her that no one wants to diagnose her, but her. She is the one constantly searching for diagnoses. She at first denies it, then quickly retracts and says it is true. HOLYMOLY. Then, she says,

> "But everyone is disagreeing on the treat-ment, and what I'M saying is no one needs to worry about me. No one. Just me and Jeff."

Okay, this seems promising! I add, "And the doctor," just to be safe.

And we agree.

Just to reassure her, I do let her know I am not trying to pry but going forward, if she calls me and begins to discuss things, I am going to give my opinion. She says this is fair and again apologizes for upsetting me, asking if I forgive her. I am SO relieved. This conversation started out horrible, I thought she was going to label me a Benedict Arnold. But all is well. It's a good day!

**Exhibit E? Do exhibits normally go on this long?**
August 12th. It's not a good day. Jillian texts me at 6:19 AM. She sends a link about "Which Disney Character Are You." Then, a text, stating "In that movie, you and Josh are the White Rabbit. The piglet. You're stressed out and wound tight. But I have a book for you to read."

This is worrisome to say the least.

Same day, but after 7 pm, Mom texts me, "Did Jeff text you too?" Jillian decided to take a half dose of the Lamictal finally, after a phone call with Mom. Okay, progress!

Shortly after, another text from Mom, "Welp that didn't last. Gracious."

Jillian texted Mom, "the Lamictal is not for me. I won't say it again."

Mom called to find out what happened and Jillian said the medication made her angry and her muscles contract. Mom notes that she is "so damn tired again." I suggest a Benadryl, thinking maybe it's an EPS type reaction? EPS is "extrapyramidal symptoms" that are most commonly found with antipsychotic use but can happen with other medications. Examples of these effects include restlessness, involuntary muscle contractions, tardive dyskinesia (involuntary facial movements), and parkinsonisms (symptoms similar to Parkinson's disease). Based on my experience, Benadryl is over the counter and will help now, but there is medication that she can take daily once prescribed, such as Cogentin.

Then, I get to thinking. I think about it all night. I think more the next day. Then I text my mom. August 13th. "I was thinking, she shouldn't have been already experiencing agitation, the half dose wouldn't have been in her yet."

**Which takes us to Exhibit F.**
August 15th. A little after midnight. Mom texts and asks if I am still awake. She asks if the Invega injection could be wearing off, it was injected on the 19th last month. I say absolutely. Jillian is supposed to be checking in with her outpatient provider tomorrow, finally. Mom suggests to Jeff that he ask to get the Invega script for the shot requested ASAP when the MD checks in.

I haven't heard about her condition in a few days, but I would be shocked that she would be willing to take an injection when she barely took a half dose of a pill a few days ago. Mom mentions that Jillian is so out of it, Jeff could say it is a vaccine and she would agree. I'm confused, she hasn't been posting, what is she doing now...

Mom says Jeff took social media off her phone, her thoughts are completely disjointed. She uprooted her plants and spread mustard/sauce on them and spread everything from the fridge into the sink before Jeff could stop her.

Fuck. Here we go again.

Mom texts later in the morning, around 9 AM. Jeff had to take Jillian back to the hospital.

This hospital stay, I don't remember being much involved. Mom was able to travel out to California this time and support on a more "in-person" basis. Thankfully, I was able to receive updates from her. I was on "Mom duty" with Jourdan.

When Jillian was out, she was clear. She was accepting.

And she was depressed.

It was so difficult to hear the updates from my mom regarding Jillian's mindset. Hearing that she felt like an alien experiment subject, that she cried talking about it all. Hearing from Jillian herself that she feels like she is trying to pilot a plane with a broken wing and she still can't differentiate between music and real life. The distress of side effects was hard enough on its own, but then add in facing the fact that she has a chronic condition on top.

And then Mom mentioned Jillian would really like to come back to Evansville for the time being.

My heart broke into a million pieces for her, because I knew that the last thing she would ever want was to come back to Evansville. She felt defeated. And there wasn't much anyone could do for her.

# CHAPTER THIRTEEN

I was back in the hospital.
  And this time, I missed my own wedding.

# JEFFREY (HUSBAND)

Dawn was almost there, and after Jillian had covered herself in more layers of clothing, I convinced her to walk with me to the hospital, although I am not sure she knew where she was going. It was all déjà vu again, only this time I had the medications Jillian was prescribed in a plastic bag to give to the medical staff for their information. I answered general questions to the best of my ability as to how she was acting, notified her family she was back in the hospital, as well as her psychiatrist's office, and walked back to the apartment to accompany Kirby, who was thoroughly confused and bereft in his own way. At least this time I promptly put together a care package with extra clothes, toothbrush, contact lenses, solution, etc.

I cleaned up as best I could. Most of the plants, even though I repotted them, ended up dying. Jillian had put the electric kettle boiler on top of the stove, and the black plastic had burned through, melting, coating, and sticking to everything. I YouTubed (it's a verb now) how to softly reheat the plastic again to make it soft and scrape it off the counters. She had randomly cut the blinds to the windows, but, fortunately, the generic blinds that came with the apartment were actually too long for the windows to begin with, so I was able to handyman a solution by cutting them down further, and it apparently worked since we totally got our full deposit back when we left at the end of our lease. I took pictures first because I didn't think Jillian would believe me about how much she trashed our apartment.

Once again, there were many calls placed to the hospital to check in with Jillian over the next couple of days, and once again I was never able to get through. At first, the staff spoke in code that Jillian was alright; they were speaking in generalities since they felt they weren't legally able to share info with me, but at a certain point they received our medical release of information form for Jillian and began sharing info with me, as well as her mother and sister.

Once again, Jillian was the one who called me three days after going into the hospital, and she seemed in good spirits, if still vague as to why she was there, expounding that she wanted to check on the place and make sure everything was alright, and I was very cautious, but she seemed to think the wedding was still on, and this was a good thing in my estimation since it meant she didn't have any plans to break up with me for committing her twice in one summer to the psych ward. However, I had also taken it upon myself to notify the wedding coordinator in Agoura Hills that Jillian was in the hospital again, and we would like to reschedule at a later time. I knew there was no way she would be in condition to coherently say, "I do," and I'm not sure how legal it is to say vows in a psychiatric ward.

Once again, they kept postponing her release date, although I was told they typically like to hold a person for three days when they are committed voluntarily; for good measure, they usually hold for longer just to be sure nothing too crazy happens when they leave. One time I was able to get ahold of a nurse to ask about Jillian since I could never get ahold of her personally, and the nurse conveyed Jillian was getting better and more cognizant and was hoping to get out in time for her wedding. Jillian was able to call me again the day before we had scheduled our wedding, hoping to get out, and I had to reassure her she just needs to get better, that we had already rescheduled once because of Covid, and we can reschedule again, trying to make it seem as though it was no big deal.

In the meantime, Brooke flew out to LA since she was already planning to attend the wedding. Unfortunately, there wasn't much she could do at this point. She couldn't visit Jillian in the hospital since the frustrating Covid regulations stipulated they wouldn't let visitors in. There were no restaurants allowing dine in, or any venues to hang around in other than the local parks, so that's basically what Brooke and I did: We'd just meet at the park and talk about Jillian, her condition, etc. while she was there. She was there to meet Jillian when she was released from the hospital, flew back to Indiana briefly, but returned to California once more, upon making the decision to extend her visit. This was welcome, as I was becoming frazzled and exhausted with it all. Kirby was always willing to help out around the place and care for Jillian, but he had no proficient command of the English language and no opposable thumbs (as well as a severe height disadvantage), so he was put in command of guarding the perimeter as well as cuddling and doggy kisses instead.

Once again, Jillian was eventually released pumped full of every psychiatric drug they could think of. When Jillian was finally able to video chat with her psychiatrist Dr. M___, the doctor had no idea Jillian had been back at the hospital; she never received any messages. She was instructed to wean herself off the plethora of drugs she had been prescribed and told to take Lithium, which is the tried-and-true drug for bipolar patients.

Incredulously, THREE WEEKS after Jillian was released from the hospital for the second time, Dr. M___ personally called Jillian and was very concerned, as her office relayed that Jillian was no longer taking her medication. Jillian replied that she was (and I could attest that she was taking her Lithium every day). It turned out that *literally a month* after notifying her office that Jillian had stopped taking her Lamictal, Dr Meg finally received the message. Another failure of the vexatious Covid regulations that the calls were always outsourced to a "virtual" office located somewhere halfway around the world? As best we understood it, there was never an office I could escort Jillian to before the ER. Dr. M___, furious at the shortcomings of the telephone operators for her practice, made it a point to give Jillian her personal number in case something like that happened again.

We ended up getting married at the end of August, and Jillian was able to walk down the makeshift aisle and not drool at all. And I formally adopted Kirby as my son.

Jillian was no longer eligible to receive unemployment, and she was no longer able to work with the severe side effects of the drugs. The doctor eventually lowered the Lithium dose when she began experiencing a metallic taste on her tongue, as well as having a hard time digesting food without getting sick. The Lithium acted like a wet blanket on every impulse, or mood, or inclination, or physical activity Jillian had. I could see why it was effective for Bipolar Disorder: it prevented any moods at all and replaced them with listlessness.

We decided it was best for Jillian if we moved back to Indiana, where she could be with family and live without the stress of LA. So we moved twice: first with Jillian and Kirby (and a lot of her personal possessions) stuffed into Jillian's car, road-tripping all through the country. Jillian even drove a little bit, after hectoring me, and it was terrifying since she still wasn't 100% in control of her fine motor skills, but we got there alive.

((Note: Jeff is always terrified of my driving, no matter how well or unwell I am. Even if I were functioning at 100%, he'd be gripping his door and what we call the "Oh shit" handle.))

I then flew back to LA and finished out my two weeks at the gas station, as well as trekking all of our major, too-big-to-fit-into-a-car stuff into storage. Our apartment manager was never in the office, due to the pretext of the frustrating and vexatious Covid regulations, so I dropped the keys into the mailbox and updated our return deposit info through text. I then trekked back again with my little Mini Cooper, from LA to Indiana, only stopping (aside from the hotel to sleep, naturally) to see the World's Largest Belt Buckle in Missouri.

# BROOKE (MOTHER)

When Jillian announces her plans to move to California, I am both excited and apprehensive. On the one hand, I want to see her chase her dreams, employing her talent and pursuing her art – what had been the focus of her life and education for a good part of her life. On the other hand, even though it has been years since her episode and struggles, California is two time zones away. Choosing to focus on her more recent thriving independence and healthiness, I push aside my concerns. It helps immensely that Jeff will be with her although I realize that his appearance in her life occurred at the end of her recovery and that it was likely that any description of that period of her life had been painted in a different light than I might have relayed. But hey, it had been years and who knows, maybe her perception was more on target than we knew.

And before long, they are there and building a life. A few weeks after they are engaged, we meet in Barstow for dinner while I am on a trip to Las Vegas. We make a longer summer visit a little over a year after they moved, Jenna, Jonah, Jourdan and I, when they were living in Panorama City. It is great fun, and she is busy and happy. She and Jeff are both on a truly positive trajectory in their acting careers.

And then the pandemic slowly takes that away. Both are fortunate to have other jobs that don't shut down and continue to pay the bills, but as their California world continues to close in tight, the stress level starts to show up in my conversations with Jillian. What I didn't know is that she had started using THC again. If I had, maybe I would have monitored our conversations more closely, parsed her words and moods differently, looking for those tell-tale signs. Of course, it may not have mattered at all.

You see, back in time as she recovered from her first bout with bipolar disorder, we had many a contentious discussion as we walked that golf course Loop regarding the role that marijuana played in precipitating her psychosis. Even after recovering with the aid of Lithium, she held tight to her belief that she likely didn't suffer from any sort of brain disease, and she was skeptical that weed played any part in her psychotic break. The Jillian of that time maintained that using weed didn't have any effect on her while at the same time insisting that it helped her sleep. No amount of pointing out the inconsistency of this line of reasoning did any good and we agreed to disagree; however, she did say that she had no intention of ever using it again and this was enough for me.

As the psychosis-free years piled up and those awful days seemed so far away, I'm sure this intention was forgotten or just didn't seem necessary anymore. Life was good, what could it hurt? And I'm not saying that this was the only or even primary cause of her more recent break, but it contributes for her, and I can't tell you how pleasantly surprised I was when reading Jillian's more recent thoughts in this book on the role that marijuana plays in putting her at risk for psychosis. This is definitely in line with what I learned from NAMI and from other multiple sources that I've read since that class in 2014.

But I didn't know she had reacquainted with this substance until her siblings started to notice, and I started to notice, those old sickeningly familiar speech patterns, and then someone spilled the beans of her THC use. A sense of foreboding began to creep in, hovering on the edges of my thoughts. And then it was all but certain as Jeff relayed her pacing and nonstop monologues.

At this point, we try to circle the wagons, Jenna providing her insight from working in the field, with Jake and me trying to support Jeff as he tangles with Jillian's increasingly bizarre exploits. The initial hope is that we can help keep her from having to be hospitalized, especially with the ramifications of COVID protocols and isolation, and then once it becomes apparent that this isn't in the cards, we try to expedite the recovery process by providing information to her healthcare team. Whether it was being so far away, more repercussions of the pandemic or just the way the mental healthcare world functions, we weren't successful in any case, as Jenna extensively covers.

Sometime before this episode, Jillian and Jeff decide to trade their Indiana wedding in October for a California wedding in August. My tax season work world is not winding down much with the postponed tax day deadline to mid-July, but I am already watching my calendar with plans to time my visit for the big day. Now, with Jillian's deteriorating health condition, I am switching gears, planning for a visit to help her and spell Jeff with a faint hope that I can still be there to witness the ceremony originally scheduled for the day after I arrived. However, it was not meant to be as Jillian remained in the hospital.

271

As a sliver of a silver lining, Jeff reinforced Jillian's good choice to make this man her life partner. As she forlornly apologizes on speakerphone for "messing up" their wedding day, Jeff assures her that they can exchange vows every day for the rest of their lives, if need be.

Game, set, match for Jeff.

Although I wouldn't wish Jillian even one more day in a hospital, it is probably good that Jeff and I have a full day to compare notes, get on the same page and sketch some plans. The first order of business is to try to help her acclimate to being back at her apartment, encouraging her to rest, a herculean task with the antipsychotic meds on board that make her fidgety, trying yoga or meditation or just short stints of quiet relaxation. Mentally she seems to be very close to baseline, but exhausted and down. On her second day home, she has a virtual appointment with her psychiatrist and, after some discussion, she agrees to put Jillian back on dependable if intolerant Lithium and suggests that it would be quite helpful if I could stay in California through the next week, mostly due to my experience with Jillian's previous episode and recovery and my knowledge of her baseline. I make a quick trip back to Indiana to gather my laptop and tie up some loose ends at the office, and then return in two days for another week.

Jillian and I spend our days together, mostly at her apartment, and I only return to my hotel in the evenings when Jeff returns home from work. In contrast to our conversations after her 2014 hospitalizations, and for months afterwards as she put her life together before moving to California, she seems to have moved away from her previous rationalizations that it was all a fluke or that it was just an overdose or some sort of one-off reaction to weed to a dawning realization that this might be something she would have to contend with for the rest of her life. At such a young age, it is overwhelming and daunting to entertain even the thought of having a chronic condition, especially after so many years with nary a sign.

But this is my second order of business, to help her accept this probability for her ultimate healing and future safety.

I remember one particular day we all went to the beach, in Malibu I think, and in a private conversation with me as we walk the surf she is angry, railing against the unfairness and pulling out any argument that she feels contradicts a diagnosis of bipolar. There is a lot of "why me" and "how could this be", all what you would expect as part of a grieving process that she has no real experience with prior to this day. So I take her figurative punches, as we parents do when needed for our children, but continue to calmly remind her of the facts, of the symptoms, trying to emphasize her relative good fortune in having such a slow cycling version that responds so successfully with the proper medicines on board. One focus is to let her use me to get it all out, not to contradict, but to redirect, just as when she or her siblings were young, remembering that she feels safe with me to put it all out there as she knows I won't cut and run. I've been all in since day one.

She is fighting valiantly. I'm reminded of days gone by, when she was just a little girl, when I would remark to her dad that one day her strength and determination would serve her well, but golly it sure would be nice if she'd just give me a break! So, I also try to use these conversations to remind her of her inner strength, how I am certain in the long run that she will be fine, even thrive again, because she is a survivor like none other, praying for her to see herself as someone of substance with more to offer the world. Easy to do because I believe every word but shared repeatedly now to try to build her up as this process of tangling with reality surely wears her down. Another one of my parenting philosophies, shared long ago with my sister, come full circle – to keep throwing mud at the proverbial wall until it sticks, meeting her determined thoughts with my own.

This wasn't the last of these conversations, but it is definitely one long step forward toward acceptance, signaled by the earnestness of her struggle. She isn't hiding this time. And it makes a strong difference too that it isn't just me and her siblings in her corner but that Jeff is there for her, too, as another person whose perspective she trusts implicitly, making difficult decisions but also in the fight with her.

If any of us were sitting on the fence about her diagnosis before, this latest episode has us all firmly across the bridge, easier for us to cross, no doubt, and we patiently wait for her to join. This book, and her reasons for writing it, are a testament to her triumph and I couldn't be prouder.

# CHAPTER FOURTEEN

Before my second hospital stay, my mother booked a flight into Los Angeles. She originally had plans to attend our wedding, but—that having been cancelled—she kept her trip on the calendar (and even extended it) to help give Jeff some much-needed relief.

He was, after all, my saving grace in California, my only (soon-to-be) relative in a stretch of nearly 2,000 miles.

The strength of this man.

Once I was discharged (I truly remember nothing from this stay beyond missing my wedding. Can't mean anything good.), my mother took over assisting me with basic tasks I'd been doing since childhood but could no longer do.

And we had a long talk about bipolar disorder.

I experienced all the stages of grief that afternoon.

That's what it finally took.

My mother talked Dr. M _ _ _ into prescribing me Lithium, and there was a significant comeback. It wasn't unaccompanied by the usual dreadful side effects, but I at least managed to find my baseline once more.

Our wedding was rescheduled for August 31, 2020, and—though my mother was now unable to attend in person—Jeff and I exchanged our vows on a beautiful, sunny hillside in a 7-minute ceremony I intend to remember forever.

Dr. M _ _ _ insisted that I be surrounded by family through the rest of my recovery. It shattered our hearts, but Jeff and I knew we had to end our magical journey in Los Angeles for the time being.

We found an apartment and were headed back to Evansville by the start of September.

Our way back was nothing short of exciting, as the dose of Lithium I was prescribed began causing a reaction akin to that of Lithium toxicity. I would wake each morning with a putrid, metallic taste coating my tongue and was unable to eat or drink anything. Not even water would stay down. There were several instances of Jeff having to pull over on an interstate in the middle of nowhere so I could hurl.

Worst. Road trip. Ever.

Thankfully, we were able to reach Dr. M _ _ _ (she allowed me to have her cell phone number since it was impossible to reach her otherwise), and she adjusted my dosage accordingly.

Back in Evansville, I temporarily crashed for a few days at my childhood home while Jeff caught a plane to Los Angeles to finish moving the majority of our belongings into a storage unit, clean our apartment, and wrap up his two weeks at the gas station.

He drove back in October, and we started over.

Bipolar disorder once again claimed victory in a crushing defeat.

Only this time, it took Jeff's dreams down with mine.

# JONAH & JOURDAN
(YOUNGEST BROTHER AND SISTER, ~~RESPECTABLY~~ *RESPECTIVELY*)

That August came with a couple of miraculous events from Jillian.

The first miracle was a phone call that I received while I was playing NBA 2k with my roommate. Jillian hadn't called in quite some time, so I had assumed she'd taken the hint. I answered this time ...

"Hey, I'm bipolar"

"Hey, yeah, I know. But it's good to hear you admit it."

We talked briefly, yet I could tell she was in fact the Jillian we all knew and...liked more than the average stranger. As opposed to the end of Episode One, it felt as though there was a sense of certainty and closure.

The second miracle is the fact that she got married. For whatever reason, I was absolutely certain at a young age that it would never happen. I nearly spoke her banishment to single, cat-ladyhood into existence, but Jeff *had* to swoop in and foil my prophecy. In all seriousness, all eyes were on Jeff throughout the second episode for multiple reasons: he was the only person in the same geographical location as Jillian, he had no prior experience of how she acted when manic, and he was the first in-law-to-be. Jeff, if you're reading this, you performed admirably, soldier. If you aren't, I take it all back and you are a mediocre husband who doesn't read their wife's book. For shame.

With the newlyweds' return to Indiana, a sense of relief yet heartbreak was ever-present in the house. Given that she had been isolated from the supportive presence of our family for so long, we rejoiced in absolute proof of Jillian's safety and well-being as she entered with what I'm sure was a joke about her own experiences and about having to stick a pin in their acting endeavors. Upon continuing to interact with Jillian, we could still tell she was not fully herself, but a zombie-like Jillian was far preferred to that which had replaced her in August. She adopted an exhausted, sullen nature about herself (and about having to stick a pin in their acting endeavors) for the next few months, but I was just happy to have my sister back.

I don't think I could definitively mark the moment I felt like Jillian returned to herself, but I honestly don't think she ever did; she became better. Although she's reclaimed much of her old self (like that beloved independence), I don't think pre-episodic Jillian can be compared to the one now. To be fair, I was very young when everything started, but the stark difference, from my perspective, seems to be her happiness. When I interact with Jillian today, she's either making others laugh in any way she can or crying-laughing 99% of the time, and I've never been happier to see her cry!

# CHAPTER FIFTEEN

I thought I knew depression, but this was a new low.

I single-handedly ruined everything we worked so hard to build, through no control of my own.

If the Lithium wasn't so good at keeping me apathetic, perhaps I'd be a puddle of tears every day. Instead I was just a hollow pit wracked with guilt.

So much better.

I began working at my mother's office again. The Lithium made it difficult to focus, absorb, and remember everything I was supposed to be doing. I only had a handful of responsibilities at first: I'd be answering phones, greeting clients as they walked in, and filing. I wasn't expected to work a full 40-hour week. A 3-hour day would drain me.

Progress was slow.

Jeff started working long, excruciating shifts at a local warehouse in order to try and recoup some of our lost finances.

There were many hours lost to exhaustion and shellshock for both of us. I would just be adding to my already pristine collection of PTSD, but Jeff was new to the experience. We kept our return to Evansville a secret to the best of our ability. The thought of trying to explain why we had to return to anyone outside of our families was … we weren't ready.

My mother requested that I speak to a therapist, and after some time I relented. I went to three sessions. At the $3^{rd}$ session, my therapist said we should delve into my trauma.

Hard pass. I didn't return.

By January of 2021, I was able to apply for Medicaid and return to seeing Dr. A _ _ _ . We picked up where we left off. He kept up my prescription of Lithium, and I kept insisting I wanted to lower my dose as much as possible. Or try something different.

After several debates, Dr. A _ _ _ decided to let me give Lamictal a whirl later that year. The same one, if you recall, that Dr. M _ _ _ had previously tried to prescribe. Only this time, Jeff and I didn't have to triangulate calls through a foreign server to try and obtain it.

Lamictal (aka Lamotrigine) is fascinating, by the way. Somewhere along the line, professionals in the scientific/medical community found that anti-convulsant drugs, mainly used to treat things like epilepsy, happen to also work as mood stabilizers.

Web MD puts it this way:

"Several anticonvulsant medications are recognized as mood stabilizers to treat or prevent mood episodes in bipolar disorder. At first, anticonvulsants were prescribed only for people who did not respond to lithium. Today, they are often prescribed alone, with lithium, or with an antipsychotic drug to control mania.

Anticonvulsants work by calming hyperactivity in the brain in various ways. For this reason, some of these drugs are used to treat epilepsy, prevent migraines, and treat other brain disorders. They are often prescribed for people who have rapid cycling -- four or more episodes of mania and depression in a year."

(https://www.webmd.com/bipolar-disorder/guide/anticonvulsant-medication#:~:text=Anticonvulsants%20work%20by%20calming%20hyperactivity,and%20depression%20in%20a%20year. )

The Lamictal was a change of pace, but one that I far preferred to Lithium. I felt much more normal; eventually my apathy dissipated, my brain fog evaporated, my focus and *most* of my memory function were restored. I took on and learned how to do more and more tasks at the office and, slowly but surely, worked my way back to my full multi-tasking capacity and a

40-hour (sometimes more during the dreaded Tax Season!) work week.

Jeff and I also became first-time home-owners in late 2021. Now able to shed the skin of our cramped apartment, I became freshly absorbed in making our brand-new house a home. The refreshed surroundings that we could call our own helped propel both of us into a more optimistic mental/emotional state.

Jeff quit the job at the factory and took on a different, more flexible job with Amazon. He would then be able to pursue a new dream—of becoming a real estate agent. He became fully licensed in April of this year (2022).

In January of this year, I started a business of my own. It most likely wouldn't have happened had it not been for a strong reaction to this remark my mother made about me at a family dinner one night:

"Paperwork is her forte."

I have zero doubt she meant it in the best way, of course. It was intended to be complimentary about my strength for com-pleting tasks (in an office setting) ef-ficiently and thoroughly that others would see as mundane. Tedious. Monotonous.

But what a depressing way of putting it.
*Paperwork* is my forte?
Gross.

My vehement reaction to her throwaway comment led me to start Organizational Consulting & Design, LLC. A professional organizing company with the moniker OCD. It was perfect.

It's still in its beginning stages. I've only been operating it for a handful of months so far. And *in this economy?* Baby, baby steps.

I also turned 30 this year, and that felt pretty ground-breaking. Fresh, new beginnings all-around have helped set in a much-needed change of pace. With that, you're pretty much caught up to the present.

Except for two things:

1.   You don't yet know my reason behind stopping my meds again and

2.   Dr. A _ _ _ fired me. Again.

The more things change, the more they stay the same.

# CHAPTER SIXTEEN

I was not fired this time on the grounds that I stopped taking my medication.

I *did* stop taking it.

But I didn't tell him this time.

My reason for stopping my meds? Jeff and I are trying to have a baby.

It was my only other goal in life that I determined when I was in college. I wanted to act, and I wanted to be a mom. Period. Those two things were all I wanted and needed to do with my life.

Bipolar disorder made both of my only goals in life distant, unattainable fantasies for some time. Miraculously, I managed to carry on and accomplish things that seemed eternally out of reach after that first hospitalization. I not only found I was able to continue acting, I even found someone willing to marry me. Insane (ha).

But you know what's still tricky about bipolar disorder? Balancing pregnancy and drugs.

The prescribed kind, to be abundantly clear.

When I spoke to Dr. A _ _ _ about conceiving, he repeatedly stressed how it was going to be a process to balance my dosage with my pregnancy. That, upon having the baby, bipolar mothers are not only capable of having postpartum depression but postpartum mania. I could have a full-blown episode right after the baby was born. And breastfeeding? Don't even get him started on how difficult that would most likely be. But Lamictal was safe. He knew loads of people who'd been pregnant on it.

M-kay.

Color me unconvinced.

I paused taking the Lamictal. Thing is, there are exponentially greater odds that my child is going to end up with bipolar disorder simply because I have it. With that already a risk on the horizon, I just want to try and give the baby as much of a fighting chance for healthy development as possible.

I asked two other doctors for their opinions on Lamictal during pregnancy. My primary care physician said, "No way José," (I'm paraphrasing), and my gynecologist assured me other women had been pregnant while taking Lamictal and delivered safe, healthy babies.

I was ready to follow up with Dr. A _ _ _ at my most recent appointment with what I'd learned from the other doctors, but he'd completely forgotten Jeff and I were trying to conceive.

Maybe it's just me, but having a baby is a pretty significant update to be aware of, especially for a bipolar patient.

This is, by the way, after the previous appointment, in which he'd referred to Jeff as my "boyfriend" and not my husband. Perhaps if he hadn't met Jeff personally, and I didn't have a completely different last name, I would not have been so skeptical.

I spoke to a phone rep at Evansville Psychiatric Associates recently about when the office would be resuming in-person appointments. Dr. A _ _ _ was still hosting ours virtually, and Covid doesn't seem to be rampaging quite the way it was years ago. Feeling that our video appointments were leading to a lack of focus and connection—on both our parts—drove me to ask:

> "I was just wondering, how long is Evansville Psychiatric Associates planning on doing these video appointments?"

> "Yes, you have a video appointment today at 3 o'clock, and it will be 15 minutes long."

(What?)

"No, I'm sorry, I meant … do you know when in-person appointments will resume at Evansville Psychiatric Associates as opposed to these virtual appointments?"

"Oh, okay, uh—"

"Are there other providers who are currently running in-person appointments?"

"Yes, there are some providers who are running in-person appointments, but Dr. A _ _ _ is doing the video appointments."

"… so, in other words, it's up to each provider whether or not they're returning to in-person appointments?"

"Yes."

So he was phoning it in. Literally. And metaphorically.

I submitted a message to the online portal, asking again about in-person appointments (just to be sure I understood correctly and in case my phone conversation with the front desk wasn't passed along) and asserting I didn't think it conducive to psychiatry appointments, given that I felt a lack of focus and connection with my provider.

And then I was fired.

According to the woman who was tasked with calling to fire me, Dr. A _ _ _ cited "underlying anger".

*sigh*

It's a frustrating and disappointing outcome, to say the least. I didn't hammer it home in my earlier chapters, but I actually really enjoyed working with Dr. A _ _ _. He's an excellent psychiatrist. We weren't always 100% in agreement, perhaps, but he was instrumental to my recovery—on more than one occasion. He was, of course, the first doctor I trusted after everything I went through prior to meeting him and the first one I sought out upon returning to Indiana. I could tell straightaway that my health was as important to him as it was to me. I don't harbor any resentment toward him, and it's unfortunate that I won't be able to work with him any longer. Sometimes that's just the way it goes.

I'm still waiting to hear back on a referral to another outpatient doctor, one that my psych-nurse-sister recommended to me. I was informed there's a minimum of 3 weeks to review a referral.

Naturally.

# JENNA (YOUNGER SISTER/ PSYCH NURSE)

To be completely clear, Jillian was not defeated. She definitely had to spend some time, upon moving back from Cali, clawing her way back to herself.

But now, she is THRIVING.

I have actually never seen a happier version of my sister than the one I see today. She and Jeff have a relationship that inspires people around them. To have a love that strong, one could only hope.

She also used to feel she could never get back into the world of acting. Let me tell you, she would absolutely still kill it onstage if she so chose. Whether she has the confidence or not, I know she could pull it out of herself.

She is constantly laughing (so obnoxiously) or making others laugh ... although she has lost her touch of making me spray drinks out of my nose. Either that, or I have gained unusual self-restraint in my abilities to hold liquids whilst laughing.

... Probably the latter, from many years practice.

We have never been closer.

And, to top it all off on all the cool things she has accomplished like being the first one of the siblings to get married, starting a business, buying a house... she is writing a BOOK!?

Working in mental health, I am so excited to see a book like this one hit the shelves. Those dealing with mental health NEED these perspectives. There is a clinical journal after a clinical perspective after more medical jargon blah blah blah about mental illness.

Enough already with the same language spun a million different ways.

People need to read real-life perspectives of those who have dealt with the illnesses. And not a single experience is the same as the next, so I hope this becomes more of the norm. It would help those dealing with the illness, whether it be the direct person or the loved ones of the person. It may even help break down some of these long-held stigmas about mental health!

So, cheers to you, Jillian. For making it through some of the toughest shit and being courageous, thoughtful, funny, and well-written enough to share your story!

# CHAPTER SEVENTEEN

I was (finally) able to meet with my new psychiatrist, Dr. R _ _ _ . He asked me about a *million* questions for a kind of getting-to-know-you ("Getting to knooooow yoooou, Getting to know allllll abooooout youuuu." Everybody! … Okay, fine, just me then.) session.

Here are some fun facts about my first appointment:

1.    Dr. R _ _ _ said, upon sending me on my merry way, that I had the *least* number of diagnoses and the *shortest* medication list of possibly any of his patients. I know, I'm as surprised as you are. To think *I'M* one of the saner ones? What is happening here.

2.    Dr. R _ _ _ believes it's entirely possible that the first hospital's diagnosis, being drug-induced-psychotic-disor-

der, could have been correct
due to the part the presence
of marijuana played in both of
my episodes thus far. With the
exception, of course, that it
was "resolved," according to the
attending physician during that
first stay. It's important to
note that these two instances
were the only times I was using marijuana regularly; though,
not in excessive amounts (Dr.
R _ _ _ assured me it may not
take much at all for someone to
have such a reaction.). Those
5+ years between my episodes, I
maybe smoked once or twice, but
it was certainly not habitual
(as it later became again, once
I thought I was home free). However, Dr. R _ _ _ is sticking to
my current diagnosis of Bipolar I until he's able to make a
clearer assessment. But certainly food for thought.

3.    Even having the LEAST number of
      diagnoses, I walked away with 3
      more (and this doesn't include
      my general anxiety): 1) OCPD-
      Obsessive Compulsive Personal-
      ity Disorder, which sounds a lot
      meaner than it actually is. It's

not the same as OCD, but we'll call it a distant cousin. If you want to know more, feel free to Google it. This diagnosis came as absolutely no surprise to me—remember the organizing business I recently started? Yeah. 2) PTSD, which everyone should know upon reading this book, that tracks. I mean, duh. And 3) Excoriation, which is a fancy word for I pick at my skin way too much.

He prescribed me one medication—Latuda (aka Lurasidone)—which is a Second-Generation Antipsychotic. He put me on the lowest dose but was leaning toward this particular drug because it:

A) Would most likely keep my episodes at bay and

B) Was the safest bet in the way of pregnancy.

Now you're officially all caught up. I have a second appointment set with Dr. R _ _ _ , but it won't be until next year (Ahaha, sorry. To clarify, that's a play on it currently being near the end of 2022. My next appointment is in early 2023. But it's in reality only 4-6 weeks. Jeff wanted to be sure I made that profusely clear. Stupid joke, I'll throw it out.).

In the meantime, I sit and stare at the blinking cursor on the screen, now trailing the letters pieced together into words, illustrating the tale of a journey that my life has unexpectedly taken.

*So is this "The End"?*

*… **does** it end here?*

I know it doesn't. This journey will last my lifetime. Every step I take into my future will be the step of someone who has had to overcome a battle most didn't know she was fighting.

Maybe it makes me crazy.

Maybe it makes me something else entirely.

*The most recent picture (that I know of, anyway)
of me with Aunt Britt. From my first professional
theatre contract ever, and just a year shy of
when my bipolar symptoms kicked in. (2013)*

*Backstage while performing in
Charlottesville, Virginia, just a few weeks
prior to first manic episode. (2014)*

At a family reunion with Jenna—this is mid-manic
episode. Note the excessive jewelry -wearing. I
hardly wear any when I'm at baseline. (2014)

This is the front cover of a workbook I
was given at the hospital in Indianapolis.
The doodles are a direct result of
mania. Don't ask me what they mean, I
haven't the slightest notion. (2014)

Annnd this is the back cover of the same
workbook. Mind you, these are just the cover
pages. The inside is *also* full of attempts to
organize and make sense of my manic brain. (2014)

*A selfie that's never seen the light of day. This was snapped during the Christmas contract I worked post first hospitalizations. You can see the weight gain very plainly in my face. (2014)*

An Easter photo I *wish* never saw the light of day (Ahem, JENNA). I'm strategically in the back left—barely recognizable by that point. Besides me, (L to R) is Jourdan, Jenna, Jacob, Joshua, Jonah, and Jules is squatting in front. (2015)

*First performance after first manic episode:
Laurey Williams in Oklahoma! at Evansville
Civic Theatre. Pictured here with some of the
cast at a promo event. Our fearless director
and friend, Kensington, in the front row
(R), Jeff is holding up his hat in the back
(L). Note: By show's end, my weight was very
close to what it was pre-episode. (2015)*

*With Jeff at rehearsal for 9to5 with Evansville Civic Theatre, after we had begun dating. (2016)*

Me (L), Jeff (Behind me), Matt (the enormously tall fellow in the back), Kensington (Front), and various cast and crew of "The Memory of Water" an Evansville Civic Theatre Underground production. (2015)

It wouldn't be right if I didn't include my
favorite photo of Kensington and myself. (2016)

During my first year at Montessori as a
Pre-Primary Classroom Assistant. (2015)

During my second year as a Pre-Primary Classroom Assistant at Montessori. (2016)

*Overlooking the ocean in Spain. I remember feeling really cool because a random Scottish gentleman at the resort told me I had an "aura" about me in his thick accent. Nothing beats hearing "aura" in a Scottish accent. (2017)*

*On the subway with Tyler after second NY audition. (2016)*

*Family Photo by Bri Schoettlin Photography. From L to R (and Birth Order): Jules (#5), Jenna (#4), Joshua (#3), Brooke (Mom), Jillian (the headcase-#2), Jourdan (#7), Jonah (#6), Jacob (#1). (2017)*

*Trip to the beach while living in LA. (2018)*

*Jeff would never forgive me if I didn't include a photo of Kirby. He is, after all, a main character ... he's just offstage. Us in front of the Hollywood sign. (2019)*

*Working as a background artist
on NBC's Superstore. (2018)*

*After being selected as a regular
background artist for Season 1 of
The L Word Generation Q (2019)*

From our engagement photo session by Melissa
Rodriguez Photography in LA. (2019)

*A photo that, again, has never seen the light of day and that—frankly—I didn't know existed until I recently found it buried in a text message exchange with my mom. Presumably snapped by Jeff at my request to show her the dress I picked out for our approaching ceremony. That I missed. Because, as you can clearly see, I was not well yet and would be hospitalized yet again. (2020)*

*Exchanging vows in Agoura Hills
immediately following second manic
episode/hospitalizations. (2020)*

*At the DuMond family Christmas. Kind of
a lost year for photos—depression and
weight struggles don't put me in the mood
to get in front of a camera. (2021)*

A photo taken in our official wedding
garb on our original wedding date. Photo
by Ingram Images, dress by Katelyn Webb &
Robert Sharkey III (college friends), bouquet
by Jeff's mother, Winda DuMond. (2020)

*Our first Easter in our first home. (2022)*

In the midst of writing this book, I (and the millions of people on TikTok and Twitter) experienced IN REAL TIME a 'celebrity' very publicly having a manic episode with psychotic features, and it still went 99.99% misunderstood almost across the board.

This internet celeb (an "influencer" on TikTok and YouTube)—a female of 31 years of age—went on a spree and uploaded over 100 TikToks in a single day. In some of them she claimed to be the second coming of Jesus (Religious Grandiosity/Delusions of Grandeur), let a man—a complete stranger—into her house, was dancing feverishly, etc. The thing that struck a chord with the public was when she began uttering things that most people would deem "racist" and "transphobic".

Here are some of the worst Twitter takes I saw:

"Having a manic episode does not excuse racist behaviour. I had a few in my life and never had I ever threw micro aggressions while having them. If it's in you it comes naturally"

"Most people experiencing psychosis would not have the personal resolve to film themselves every time they go thru an episode. She has borderline personality disorder or BP1 possibly. She could not maintain her lifestyle if she were really experiencing psychosis. It's a farce."

"she's just trying to be popular again come on"

"White women love to weaponize their mental state as an excuse to be flat out ignorant I cannot say that I am shocked"

"Agreed. I'm severely I'll [sic] and have psychotic breaks on the reg. Racism isn't my go to because I'm not a racist. Your worst traits come out when you have breaks. This is just her showing who she is…"

"mental health issues isn't an excuse for making racist or transphobic comments."

"Medication exists. No sympathy. Sincerely, a bipolar person who nearly destroyed his family."

"No I don't think you get what I'm saying. She didn't say a crazy thing she said a racist thing. Yes she [sic] not mentally right but let's not be dense and deny that she say [sic] some racist and messed up shit"

"As someone who has manic episodes very similar to G___, yes she can control herself online. Especially if she's aware of her mental illness. You learn the signs of a manic episode coming. You learn how to be proactive to not say and do things you don't mean caused by delusions."

"Social media isn't the place to rant when your [sic] having an episode. She needs therapy and she obviously knows that by now. It's common sense at this point. She has said some cruel dehumanizing things before that were ignored all because she's crazy. Of course."

"so many people are trying to defend her because she's mentally ill, but forget that illnesses like that just bring your true self out more. i've seen it happen and would excuse it, just to find out that's just who they are. she's been begged to get help for YEARS & she refuses"

"There are millions of people with mental issues and yet they manage to not be racist or insulting to anyone. She could've gotten help , mental issues or depression don't come over night."

"It's true but many people with mental health issue [sic] don't say anything transphobic and racist shit either. If her mental health is that bad I think someone who's close to her should get involved."

"She should've gotten help and medicated when first diagnosed. She's racist and needs to be held accountable for her actions instead of being coddled like a child."

"Mental illness doesn't cause racism and transphobia. That's like saying taking Ambien causes racism (ROSEANNE)"

"Bro thinks imma let [sic] here and let someone be racist just because their brain isn't braining"

"I understand G___ H___ is having a manic/psychotic episode but when r [are] we gonna stop excusing harmful words & behaviors in the name of "mental health crisis" – white privilege is being able to blame racist, homophobic & transphobic rants on mental health with 0 accountability"

"She's been like this for years babe stop making excuses for her if she wanted help during times when she was stable she would've gotten it you can't help someone who doesn't want it."

"my thoughts exactly. I'm so tired of seeing people get mad at those who are getting upset about her horrible rants. like yes it sucks like she's having a breakdown and I sincerely hope she gets the help she needs but like we're also allowed to be mad about the things she's saying"

"For freaking real because I'm not really sure what poor mental health and being any sort of bigot have to do with one another! You can go into panic mode without being an asshole"

"Worked in a psych hospital and they taught in training that if a patient is verbally abusive through racist or homophobic comments, you can report it because if they understand enough to know what racist or homophobic thing to say that would offend you, they're responsible. As in, if for example they see I'm a Muslim and make an [I]slamophobic comment, they understand enough to be somewhat held accountable."

"I'm saying that she should be held accountable for saying awful things about vulnerable people with a platform of millions of people, an alcoholic should still be held accountable for drunk driving even tho [though] alcoholism is a disease/ addiction ya know?"

"It sincerely does not matter if she's in a manic episode or not – the things she has said are harmful and she needs to be held accountable. To let her get away with this, is to taint the reputation of those with bipolar disorders. We are not crazy and out of control. She is."

"I'm tired of people like her and T__ you can't hide behind illness making you a bigot"

"[W]hen im manic i don't go on racist rants. mania doesnt make you racist, it just gets rid of the filter you have. shes clearly always had these bigoted thoughts, the mania just let them come out"

Suffice it to say, the general public still has no understanding of bipolar disorder, mania, manic episodes, psychosis, etc.

Thankfully, there were sensible and supportive comments interspersed through-out the mudslinging, so let's don't lose all hope:

> "And some of the replies under this thread prove your point – people really don't know a thing about psychosis and also how difficult it can be to get someone into a facility if they are unwilling. It's all just really sad esp bc [especially because] it's playing out in front of millions."

> "Actually, it's a pretty valid excuse. Rationality goes out the window when you're in the midst of an episode. Doesn't make the behaviour ac-ceptable, but y'all need to put down your fucking pitchforks."

> "What the fuck are you talking about? Do you know what a psychotic break is? Do you know what it entails? Anyone trying to hold her ac-countable for what she says and does right now is more psychotic than she is."

> "While what she said was completely inexcus-able, I think a lot of you commenting this have never actually experienced someone in psycho-sis. 9/10 she may not remember this until she sees the video, if and when she comes out of it."

> "I don't think you understand exactly what a man-ic episode does to someone. You think things you don't normally do [sic] and you say things

you don't ACTUALLY believe. She is going to come out of this scared, just have some sympathy for her instead of thinking about yourself"

"Literally no one here said that mentel [sic] illness is an excuse for the things she said. But y'all just straight up have 0 understanding of what it's like to experience a break from reality. Shut up for 2 seconds and listen to mentally ill people telling you that you're not helping … . G____ won't see or care about what you have to say, but the people around you with similar mental health issues will."

"my grandpa was bipolar and also thought he was the second coming of jesus and he tried to kill his whole family multiple times, and ppl r tryna [people are trying to] cancel her, she literally doesn't understand what shes [sic] doing is wrong."

"It's terrifying what I saw , feeling that on top is only going to be so hard when she eventually comes crashing down. I know she says she's ok but when your [sic] like that your [sic] not thinking clearly even if you think you are. I really hope she gets the help when she's ready."

"Idk [I don't know] who G____ is but I used to work in acute psych care and manic ppl [people] are in a very vulnerable state—seen pts [patients] unable to say coherent sentences, stripping naked & running around, eating soap, having god-like delusions, switching from screaming/laughing/ sobbing in a 5 sec span … . I mean, I once I [sic] had a very delusional pt [patient] say he would kill me and eat my genitals. Mental illness is wild. I'm not defending any awful things this person said but if she is in a manic/delusional state she is likely to be saying indefensible things"

"My uncle was bi-polar (he's passed now) and when he took his medication, he was fine. He was so fine that he thought he didn't need to take them anymore. Then he would be manic. It got so bad that his friends would come over for coffee everyday [sic] to make sure he took his meds. I [w]ish people would have a heart. Some ppl [people] are delusional or can't see they need help. Some of them feel helpless or scared. I personally know I need help with my mental illness, but my illness is holding me back. It's not always about not wanting help."

"People always claim to be a mental health advocate UNTILL [sic] MENTAL HEALTH THINGS ACTUALLY HAPPEN"

"If someone is deluded and hallucinating then they don't owe you an apology. It is upto [sic] you as the sane person to be the bigger person and simply get over it and realise that their words have no meaning and they have no idea what they are saying. They are very very poorly."

"You have no grasp of mental health issues, the tweets some of you are putting out are ridiculous. Do we start cancelling people suffering with Tourette's syndrome next? In no way is she of sound mind, she has lost touch with reality and you're out here like "sHe NeEdS to PaY!"

"She's literally not in the right state of mind. Court wouldn't hold her accountable for her actions what makes you think YOU can"

"not everyone has the mental awareness and this might be her first episode. i completely lost myself in psychosis, did all the things G___'s doing, and damaged everyone around me. i had No control over what i was doing and we should stop assuming that she does until she's better"

"I am not supporting G___ H___. I made it clear I'm not a fan. I'm supporting others with these issues that are having their mental health mocked and decided for them. I stated that it was possible for someone to say uncharacteristic things during these episodes. Which is true."

"Thank you for getting it. So many armchair experts coming out of the woodwork today that have had a panic attack or something so they think they understand severe mental illness. Meanwhile anyone who's gone through it or worked in mental health KNOWS. How severe a break can look. Complete deviation from normal self."

"yeah i also can't help but feel like being literally in a state of psychosis is probably a valid excuse for saying problematic things"

"Our court system literally recognizes people in this state are not fully responsible for murder in the same way as others and y'all are losing your shit over some racist statements she probably barely understands right now."

"That's your experience, not everyone's. Should it be forgotten? No. Sometimes they aren't aware. My mom thought I was possessed. She tried to attack me to get back [sic] her daughter back. She was so upset when she came out of it that she tried to kill herself. One size doesn't fit all."

"I've literally thought I was being hunted by birds that were spying on me during mania. Mania and psychosis can be entirely irrational and nothing to do with your actual stable self. Don't project your experiences on to [sic] all of us"

"I'm not a huge fan of G___ H___, however, people that say episodes of mania or psycho-sis can't cause you to say things you wouldn't normally have never seen the worst. I saw my mother become a [sic] unrecognizable person during episodes and that was never who she was. Be better."

"no seriously last year when i had my psychotic break i refused help i truly didn't think i needed it"

323

"yeah, regardless of how you feel about g___
h___ and all the shit she's done in the past, can
we please stop saying that people reveal their
true, "deep down" feelings when they're manic?
it's inaccurate and unhelpful"

"It's so hard dealing with people during mania.
They feel like they're seeing clearly for the first
time EVER and you can't get through to them
no matter how much you plead."

"People DO NOT care about mental health
as much as they do online. They only scratch
the surface and look at infographics unless it's
someone close to them, but even then! Sometimes they don't do the research& they will 100%
make the person suffering the villain [w]hich al-
lows them to avoid accountability & STIGMA-
TISE mental health further."

"No one is excusing her actions, but if you really
think you should hold a clearly mentally unwell
person accountable in the middle of them being basically detached from reality, your view of
mental illness is clearly somehow skewed. She
needs help rn [right now]. not an interrogation."

"Pretending to care about mental health and then
demanding people suffering a psychotic break,
whose thoughts are literally incoherent, take accountability for the whacky stuff their sick brain
is making them say isn't a good look."

"My mum was so delusional when she had psychosis it was only the shell of her that was left. She would say things to me she would never say as her normal self. Psychosis is an incredibly difficult thing to go through."

"Fucking thank you but people are so shitbrained in a legitimate mental health crisis when there's multiple resources of info for them to learn from … I've noticed society is always so easy [sic] eager to revoke empathy no matter the situation. Clinging onto useless pieces of info or thought processes in an attempt to delegitimize someone who is a victim."

"happened to someone close to me, that shit really takes the earth out from under your feet, some people lose everything, due to something they have no control over … . It can take months-YEARS to fully recover from psychosis; if you're lucky enough to make a full recovery, slipping in and out of reality; and not remembering gaps in time, shits [sic] no joke, it's not a "haha ur crazy ;P" situation"

"When you're in mania with psychotic features you don't actually believe you need help and a lot of the times mania feels good (euphoric) … I watched a few videos and she has grandiosity, religiosity (claims she's the second coming of Jesus in one video), flight of ideas, etc etc… . I genuinely do not know her before/outside of this. Her racist and transphobic shit aside, she needs inpatient treatment. We're watching psychosis in real time and it's sad. I hope for her sake she has loved ones that care and are trying to arrange help for her."

"she's clearly having religious grandeur delusions she thinks she's the next jesus it's a pretty common symptom that indicates mental health problems and she needs to get help right away"

"Girlie was laughing at people who were worried saying crap like "why would you be worried about the happiest person on earth" or some crap … . People saying she needs to stop and get help like she can just "OKAY BRAIN THAT'S ENOUGH" are dense"

"People in these psychosis states don't understand reality. Why would she ask for help if she doesn't think anything is wrong? In her mind right now, this is normal. It's an Illness."

" "if she wanted help she'd get it" like people are failing to understand she probably doesn't even recognize that she needs it – the lack of empathy people manage to show is astounding and the internet is brainwashing people into using these things as entertainment"

" "Mental illness is no excuse for being racist" It can literally lead to murder, suicide, and believing you are god but ok."

"People don't understand that she thinks she's the second coming of Jesus rn [right now]. In psychosis people are irrational, unintelligible, violent, hallucinating. She doesn't know wtf [what the fuck] she's doing."

"yes the sad truth is that these things are not so simple to prevent. i had a family friend that was diagnosed with bipolar in his 40s and prescribed medication. he had a severe reaction to it leading to psychosis. he tried to kill his wife, police got involed [sic], and he was killed"

"I'm convinced that most people really don't even understand depression and anxiety lol [laugh out loud], they confuse depression with being sad and anxiety with being nervous and what not [sic], a lot of people basically use it synanumously [sic]. But they sure as heck don't understand shit beyond that"

"I know nothing of this story or why it's on my feed but until you watch a loved one go through a manic episode it's almost impossible to understand what it really is like hopefully this person has a good support system to help them through it."

"The fact the tea [slang for gossip] community talks about other humans as if they have somehow mastered psychology and are better than them is both disturbing and disgusting. But hey get that clout"

"Fr [For real]. My sister suffers from manic episodes. You guys are so all there for struggling with mental illness until it gets real [sic] ugly and doesn't fit your aesthetic. She has NO SENSE of reality and she's potentially in danger. The girl needs help."

"It's not about supporting G___. I don't support her at all; I've never followed her. It's about understanding that she's struggling with severe mental illness, and people are saying very damaging, stigmatizing things about mental health & mania."

"you guys have too much faith in the medical model and the current state of mental health care. it's not a magic fix. even going to therapy and doing everything "right" can still lead to things like this. it's easy to say "get help" but the sad reality is that it's not that simple"

"A lot of people are not ready for the reality of untreated mental health issues & it shows"

"It makes me sick to see how many people are using her for content. Like oh, let me add cute music to your mental health crisis."

"people are joking about refreshing g___ h___'s tiktok so they can "keep up" with her videos while she goes through a public mental health crisis. a random guy entered her home, and is now talking about her on live with 16k viewers. all of this is so voyeuristic and gross…. . social media gives the public unprecedented access to creators but people in crisis are not entertainment"

"ya'll [sic] taking words that she's saying while in a [sic] EPISODE OF PSYCHOSIS, & twisting them to mean whatever you want to make them mean – is fucking gross. educate yourself on psychosis. she doesn't know how 2 [to] articulate what she is *actually* trying to say bc [because] she has broken away from reality. you're interpreting what she is saying in your own fucking way and then holding it against her. she is not currently making sense bc [because] she is experiencing psychosis. she has no control over the phrases and words she is using. for fucks sake yall [sic] are so daft."

"This is false information and you should stop spreading it. Mental illness doesn't bring your 'true self' out. That is completely false and shows your intentions. People are defending her bc [because] holding someone accountable during an episode will not help. There is a time and place"

"Tysm [Thank you so much] I've experienced med [medication] induced psychosis due to medical malpractice before and it's been 3 years and I've never been the same. My heart hurts for her even if she's problematic and hard to like in normal situations. My heart hurts"

"If someone can go on rants about how they are literally god why does it not make sense that they'd also say something racist??? People seem to pick and choose what to take seriously from someone going through a mental breakdown"

"Thank you for saying this, it's also similar to someone with Tourette's saying awful things. They quite literally can't control what they are saying. G___ is just spewing nonsenses that her brain had heard before and has nothing to do with what she believes."

"You know when people having manic episodes start talking about aliens or conspiracy theories, even make up scenarios. Mania is very debilitating, it can lead to dissociation in which that person does not know what they are saying and won't remember"

"people can literally think they can do stuff like photosynthesize or something during manic episodes, let's not try to treat anything they say like they're in a normal state of mind because g___ currently thinks her backyard is the garden of eve [sic]"

"I remember my mother having a manic episode so bad once she told me she regretted me so bad, she wanted me to die. She didn't even know she was taking [sic] to me. If she apologises,

forgive it, she's not aware of what she's saying. If not, then say this"

"We just gonna mock severe mental illness then aye? Glad society has progressed since the last influencer killed themselves."

"She's having a psychotic episode besties, making fun of her mania and her delusions is not the best look"

"A couple of months ago, something similar happened to a close friend of mind (but wasn't on a platform of 7.4M followers). Not sleeping, making grandoise [sic] claims like this. She is absolutely in crisis and needs help right now. I hope her family can get her the help she needs."

"Sounds like mania. Mania is really horrible and yes it can change the way you feel and the way that you think. It's not always so extreme. I would just feel really bad for her, recovery is going to hurt a lot."

"She's having a manic episode and people are trying so hard to cancel her … y'all do know manic episodes have people saying things they don't really mean?? Like it's intrusive thoughts and she really can't help it … . She is having a MANIC episode, she isn't herself. She's genuinely mentally ill. A MANIC person goes through psychosis, Psychotic episodes occurring during mania and can cause a person to become delusional or hallucinate. So no, she can't : / /"

"People don't understand bipolar at all."

No, no they do not. But thankfully, there are many people online (and better yet, in the real world) who *do* understand it and are fiercely advocating for those who go through it.

Always remember: No one is alone.